Customer-Driven Operations

Customer-Driven Operations

Aligning Quality Tools and Business Processes for Customer Excellence

Christopher Ahoy

New York Chicago San Francisco Lisbon London Madrid Mexico City
Milan New Delhi San Juan Seoul Singapore Sydney Toronto

The McGraw·Hill Companies

1 2 3 4 5 6 7 8 9 0   DOC/DOC   0 1 0 9 8

ISBN-13: 978-0-07-160831-2
ISBN-10: 0-07-160831-1

This publication is designed to provide accurate and authoritative information in regard to the subject matter covered. It is sold with the understanding that the publisher is not engaged in rendering legal, accounting, or other professional service. If legal advice or other expert assistance is required, the services of a competent professional person should be sought.

> *—From a declaration of principles jointly adopted by a committee of the American Bar Association and a committee of publishers and associations.*

McGraw-Hill books are available at special quantity discounts to use as premiums and sales promotions, or for use in corporate training programs. To contact a representative, please visit the Contact Us pages at www.mhprofessional.com

This book is printed on a acid-free paper.

To all my family and friends and to all those
who asked me to write this book

Contents

Acknowledgments

SINCERE APPRECIATION GOES TO MY WIFE, Ruth, for putting up with the many evening and weekend hours when I busily focused on writing this book (which began in 2003). Thanks to my two editors, Ruth Ahoy and Kenneth Lynn, for giving me endless hours of their time. Thanks to Lauren Lynch, assistant editor, and Scott Kurtz, production editor, McGraw-Hill, for the final touches to this book.

To all those who supported my endeavors and initiatives in the many places of my work life where I was privileged to lead five private and public organizations of very talented and dedicated groups, I thank you. My deep appreciation to many friends and colleagues for asking me to make a presentation at their companies, institutions, and conferences, which has continued to spark my enthusiasm in compiling this book. My heartfelt appreciation and thanks to all of you for patiently listening to my ideas on the concepts of becoming a world-class operation.

"Tashi Delay" in Tibetan means, "I honor the greatness in all of you."

Christopher K. Ahoy
Ames, Iowa 2008

Preface

"IN A WORLD populated with the regular and the ordinary so distastefully hyped to unimaginable levels of stature and reverence, your organization and its seemingly impossible accomplishments are . . . well . . . they're more inspiring than you can imagine. The vision, foresight and single-mindedness of your efforts and those of your colleagues are, if you'll pardon the cliché, amazing. And especially heartwarming to me is the level of genuine enthusiasm and pride you take in the well-deserved success you and the organization have achieved, though it does belie the extensive amount of energy everyone has expended to get you to the place you are. How fortunate for ISU your orbits crossed when they did—and how fortunate for the rest of us here in central Iowa we have someone of your stature right here in the 'hood as a colleague and unselfish contributor to our collective body of wisdom and experience of all things related to quality. . . . I look forward to learning more from you the next time our own paths cross. . . . Until then, stay the course—you're definitely on the right path."

William E. Harris III, Director of Quality
ITA, Group Inc.,
January 12, 2006

WHY THIS BOOK?

By special demand! At my presentations, many attendees would ask, "Where's the book?" I began writing late in the evenings after work beginning in 2003 and completed the first version in the spring of 2005. This is the final version.

Many have played a role in helping and urging me to write a book on what it takes to create a world-class organization. This book, *Customer-Driven Operations: Aligning Quality Tools and Business Processes for Customer Excellence*, is based on my lecture series. The initial intent of the lecture series was to educate staff members in the precepts of becoming the best they could be. I laid a foundation at the outset by developing a road map for our successes in a 12-year quality journey in the Facilities Planning and Management Department at Iowa State University. (See www.fpm.iastate.edu/worldclass.)

I faced many problems and issues in driving solutions, which I later learned were the same solutions many other organizations were seeking. The initiatives we put in place were in support of Iowa State University's aspiration to become one of the best land grant institutions in the nation and one of the leading teaching and research institutions in the world in science and technology. These same initiatives appear to be ones needed by most other organizations aspiring to reach the pinnacle of success in becoming a world-class operation. At my many presentation venues my audience would ask, "How do we implement the processes that lead to a world-class organization?"

I learned many lessons during the course of implementing the best practices by following a persistent, consistent, clear, and compelling vision for transformation. I was fortunate to be in the right place at the right time. These circumstances helped me to formulate a theory and practice. The central focus has been to share the concepts of achieving world-class stature through "raising the bar" of high performance throughout the world. To engage with individuals seeking this pinnacle of success creates an atmosphere charged with excitement. Many changes are possible by leveraging technology and using appropriate classic quality tools that fit any organization. Teaching and coaching an organization requires a clear vision of the future based on values. You teach employees and they teach each other, which solidifies their own knowledge.

Taking an organization through a value-based, organization-design, high-level, relationship-building journey is well worth-while. It is my belief that any organization aspiring to become the best will have a competitive advantage over the competition. In a global economy, a competitive advantage is important. When an organization is moving from the survival mode to one that is thriv-ing, it must have an agility that is primed to constantly shift its shape. Knowing just how is the key to creating a world-class oper-ation to reach "customer success."

I introduced paradigm shifts into our staff's thinking and behav-ior; made cultural changes through many initiatives in the processes of continuous quality improvement and transformational method-ologies; and changed the focus to processes rather than tasks. By leveraging technology, I made process improvements and moved our organization forward. (See Chapter 4 in this book.) This lever-aging made possible the successes the department achieved by using continuous quality improvement and it also mitigated some of the resistance and the challenges posed by our "culture keep-ers"—employees whose mindset includes "if it works now, why change it?"

The processes used in the journey resulted in many inquisitive visitors coming to the Facilities Planning and Management Department, and making requests for information on how to attain world-class stature. As I shared our information with other organizations, they began their own continuous quality improve-ment journey to develop their own world-class operatives to fill their "gaps." The feedback from colleagues and the recognition and appreciation for achieving successes in our quest brought additional visits to our ISU site and personal invitations to speak at many venues. We received many testimonials, accolades, recogni-tions, and awards along the way.

Since Iowa State University is a not-for-profit organization, we share our information freely. The sharing we do with various enterprises verifies that we are on the right track and moves us to continue our journey. That many people want to hear more about our "quest to become the best" boosts our energy to keep on doing what we do in the best interests of our parent organization (ISU) and ourselves.

> *"When an organizations starts to question what it does and why it does it, it can begin to lay a 'yellow brick road' that will lead to its own long-term goals toward achieving the pinnacle of success."*
> Seminars—Creating Awareness for a
> World-Class Operation
> Ahoy, 1997–2007

As you navigate through this book, you will see that we have followed this road.

CHAPTER

Where Does a World-Class Journey Begin?

> *"The reward of the young scientist is the emotional thrill of being the first person in the history of the world to see something or to understand something. Nothing can compare with that experience.... The reward of the old scientist is the sense of having seen a vague sketch grow into a masterly landscape."*
> Cecilia Payne-Gaposchkin[1]

WHERE THE JOURNEY BEGAN

In the spring of 1997, Iowa State University's (ISU) Facilities Planning and Management (FP&M) department began a 12-year quality journey to become a world-class operation. We devised a systemic way of looking at our organizational development involving system thinking and empowerment for our people. The task lay in establishing a direction for the organization to proceed into the future with a stated vision, mission, and core values. For my staff, I chose a flatter organization at the outset, away from the traditional top-down command and control structure. I discovered that through pathfinding (alignment of the organization by looking at the system in its parts and as a whole) and by working on empowering people (finding a home for their talents and creating a safe environment), our people's talents would flourish through volunteerism rather than conscription.

I focused on strengths and coped with our weaknesses while we moved away from a task focus to a process focus. I created a value-based organization by changing our culture through leveraging technology. Small groups can sometimes leverage effectiveness. We brought process improvement methodology aboard to help with cultural lag. We brought process improvement to the culture, not the culture to the process. I developed materials for several classes and wrote several articles to assist staff in explaining where we were going and why. The class presentations were geared to create awareness for a world-class operation and to gain the knowledge and skills necessary to engender workers to meet the challenges that lay ahead.

To create the desired high-level performance, I met individually with our staff members, as well as with members of peer institutions, professional associations, and other enterprises—private and public entities—in the process to create awareness for world-class operations. These meetings increased the number of those interested in creating a world-class operation and inspired many others to create world-class operations of their own. Interest in this subject matter has persisted and continues to demand a common source for information. People continually ask me to make this information available in written form, and they invite me to speak at their conferences throughout the world. These presentations created a hunger among individuals and audiences as a whole for a high level of performance in their own organizations.

It became evident that the various initiatives that I was inculcating into my own organization were not just what my organization needed, but what others of similar inclination were seeking. Questions posed during these presentations were as follows:

1. How did you create the organizational climate for quality?
2. How were the quality visions articulated in your strategic plan?
3. What were the key drivers that pushed the vision with the core operation of the organization?
4. How do you measure individual and organizational performance and core competency?
5. What kinds of initiatives, objectives, and targets were put in place?

Whatever the methodology an organization uses for capturing its market share of customers, the primary focus of marketing is to test the waters of its competition to see what the organization must do to be in a position to heed the voice of the employees and the voice of the customers to meet or exceed its customers' focus (see Chapters 6 and 7). Many people had a hand in developing the processes, but it has not been the practice for a single individual or department to be accountable for the overall process results. In a process-centered approach it is possible to remove the nonfunctional silos and look at complexity, fragmentation, lack of technology, layers of approval, lack of a process owner, redundancy, number of forms, degree of customer focus, cost of non-value-added activities, number of hand-offs, and the reworking of some subprocesses.

The question often crops up, "Which should we be more concerned about, the quality of our products or services, or the quality of our business process?" Customers are five times more likely to be adversely affected by poor business results because of a *defective process* than by poor products and services, i.e., lack of ownership of an activity process and too many handoffs within the organization.

A process is a series of activities and events. Proper management comprises the art of handling the processes and using measurement tools to determine improvement over baseline performances. In a supply chain, or value stream, the process begins with the supplier and ends with the customer. Generally known as a *value stream*, the supplier, input, process, and customer are a chain-linked, continuous operation in a linear direction. A process has a beginning and an end. A process consumes resources and requires standards for unbiased repeatable performance measurements. It responds to control systems that direct the quality, rate, and cost performances of an organization. To achieve a competitive advantage, we must monitor our processes constantly for improvement.

As Peter W. Keen wrote in the *Process Edge*, "Processes are the source of 'firm-specific' special competence that makes the competitive difference."[2] There is no product or service without a process. Likewise, there is no process without a product or service. Process makes the organization. Some basic considerations of how an organization can better its processes are:

1. Consider doing the "right things" rather than just doing "things right."
2. Eliminate unnecessary steps to conserve resources.
3. Ask better questions to get better answers.
4. Evoke moving processes faster, better, smarter, and less expensively.
5. Ask, are we protecting "sacred cows" that inhibit change and limit our success?
6. Look for the hidden factors.
7. Convert inputs into results (outputs).
8. Require standards for repeatable performances.
9. Respond to control systems, which direct the quality, rate, and cost of performance.

At the process end of the organization, the members are focused on the essential concepts, methods, and tools needed to successfully manage work processes. These are the worker bees of the organization interested in producing the best products and services that they know how. It has been said that at the Toyota factory, as well as in other enlightened manufacturing process organizations, the process level worker is empowered to stop the system if there is evidence of any flaw. Such a methodology is called *error-proofing*, or the Japanese term *poka-yoke*.

At the process level, the workplace organizational principles are clear and well understood. Workers are emotionally connected to key priorities set by the operations management leadership. Most translations must be made easy so the "line of sight" from job, team, etc., to key priorities is unobstructed to avoid mistakes and frustrations. Individuals and teams must be disciplined, diligent, and empowered workers with knowledge, capability, and capacity to perform the task for which they are trained—to take the "is" condition to the next level of excellence. Managers must remove roadblocks (this could include structural as well as cultural systems) that may have existed from time immemorial. Removing roadblocks will be the responsibility for both the top echelons and the process operational mangers. Most process owners work best in a collaborative, synergistically working environment with trust and accountability to each other; and they are responsive to achieving prioritized goals. For process mapping from the current reality condition to the future state to the ideal state, see the next few pages.

You must create the situation for transformation through *organization design* (see Chapter 8). This is an approach to organization structures, incentive systems, business process design, operational fixes, and process improvement methodologies for promoting people. It guides the changing culture to the understanding of globalization, cultural diversity, intellectual capital, and knowledge capital; and it creates awareness of the limited resources on our planet through resource management.

Almost everything a company or organization does involves a *process*. In fact, everything that we do in our lives involves a process. "A process is any activity or group of activities that takes an input, adds value to it, and provides an output to an internal or external customer."[3] In a process mode, a management philosophy is needed to set the direction of an organization. Creating a total quality management philosophy for the organization helps to gear employees in their paths toward success.

Total quality management (TQM) became very popular, and it swept across all the industrial sectors. Although TQM is still valid with incremental improvement, it lacks the measures that processes demand in today's industrial and commercial sectors. For a while business process reengineering took its place, and became a more refined process improvement approach that leverages information technology to manifest improvements through a data-driven culture across cross-functional boundaries. Organizations that focus only on cost cutting and downsizing do not last long. "A completely different thought pattern occurs when you focus on the process."[4]

Many of today's processes are in a sad state. Processes are fragmented across isolated functional departments. Processes are plagued by numerous organizational handoffs. Individuals cannot be held accountable without having the "whole story" needed to make corrections to the process. Handoffs are the source of non-value-added work, creating delays, errors, and inflexibility because:

1. Those involved in the process cannot see or understand the whole endeavor.
2. The process or a subprocess is invisible, unmeasured, and unmanaged.
3. No one has accountability or management responsibility.
4. Different offices or work units view each other with suspicion

The first step in resolving these problems is process mapping.

PROCESS MAPPING

Process mapping is a method of understanding a process thoroughly. It is the most commonly used quality tool for checking the "as is" condition of an organization or process—from current reality, to future state, to the ideal state. It is a tool for analyzing and improvising business processes by determining the current reality and making improvements leading to the future state and ultimately to the ideal state. Mapping a process in a world-class operation is critical to determining the existing conditions.

Process mapping assists in developing professional performance measures and targets, which in turn signals how well individual activities are contributing to a particular process. Activities discovered through process mapping reveal linkages among organizational resources and the products and services produced and delivered to the customers. It would be difficult to emulate best practices without putting the process language in place in an organization and using statistics as a means of measuring progress. The reason for focusing on process is to create an awareness of what a world-class operation really is. This quest to become the best begins with three precepts—attitude, process, and tools. These are discussed in more detail in Chapter 2. The endeavor to move an organization to become a world-class operation must start by creating an awareness of world-class culture and by looking at the world-class paradigms of attitude, process, and tools that are necessary in pursuing the journey to achieve excellence and in seeking greatness through outstanding results.

The Process Map

A *process map* is a picture of a business process or system sufficiently detailed to facilitate meaningful improvements. The map is the most important quality tool in a process. By mapping existing processes into a flow chart, the map becomes the main thrust in understanding the sequences of activities in defining the current reality state or the "is" condition, and in determining where the organization "should be" in the future state, before moving into the "could be" condition which is the ideal state. The current (is) condition is derived from the "pissed-off line" (PO'd line), which is the bottom line for any organizational modus operandi.

See Figures 6.1, 6.2, and 7.2. This is the minimal condition that any customer is expected to tolerate as the basis for moving upward into becoming an outstanding organization.

The technique of mapping provides a critical analysis for defining performance issues and for understanding the voice of the customer and supplier requirements. The following are four different types of process maps:

1. Relationship map
2. Cross-functional process map
3. Linear process map
4. Job/task process map

To understand the current reality of how business is conducted, an organization must map its existing as-is processes and then determine where its future and ideal states are.

Mapping the Existing Processes

We must map an existing process to obtain a better understanding of our critical business factors. We must modify this map to take our organization to the next level of excellence by raising the bar. To achieve a competitive advantage, mapping a process must be monitored constantly for improvement. Mapping the current reality (the "is" condition) provides help to the organization for making the decision of the organization's "should be" condition (the future state). Mapping and designing the desired state will lead to the "could be" condition (the ideal state) and world-class operatives.

It is important to process map each work unit's current state operatives to determine how existing practices function. All these exercises should be done to determine the gap analyses, where we need to go from where we were in the current state of affairs—from current reality, which is the "is" condition, before proceeding to the should-be condition, or the must-be condition, or the can-be situation. To understand the current condition, we mapped many processes in our organization, looking at work in process in every aspect of the organization's modus operandi. Once we determined the current reality, we could then find the root causes for the existing conditions that did not function well or that did not operate efficiently. Then we determined what corrective and preventative actions we need to take. By identifying those issues in each of our processes, and by understanding clearly what we needed to do to take each of the work units to operational excellence, we were able to create the required "metric" to track what mattered most in our operations. If you can't track it, you can't measure it. The mapping technique is available on ISU's Web site at http://www.fpm.iastate.edu/worldclass/process_mapping.asp and also from sources listed in Chapter 11.

THE PROCESS OWNER

Process owners are the managers of a business unit or personnel that are key to the operations of the organization because of their subject matter expertise. The process owner who makes the marketing pitch for any particular process in the organization has end-to-end responsibility for that process, its performance, and any changes made to that process. The process owner:

1. Creates the design of the process.
2. Specifies the steps and how they fit together.
3. Notes that the design must be evolving rather than static.
4. Assures that the design is updated on an ongoing basis to keep up with changing customer demands and competitive pressures.
5. Establishes the measurement system for the process.
6. Offers guidance to the people who perform the process by assisting them when they ask for it.
7. Is an advocate for the process by obtaining needed resources and represents the process in corporate decision making.

The traditional organization has its benefits. People merely have to follow their bosses' orders, which give them a significant degree of clarity and make their lives relatively simple. To support the new organization, the management systems (for budgeting, planning, and the like) must be realigned from function to process. Hence there has to be a process to explain what we do and how we do things.

> *"The process of consistently researching for new ideas or methods, practices and processes and either adopting the new practices or adopting the good features and implementing them to become the best of the best."*
>
> Robert C. Camp,
> Xerox Corporation

BENCHMARKING

A benchmark is defined as a point of reference from which measurements may be made, something that serves as a standard by which others may measure. The term can refer to a particular point within a series of processes that is a good stopping point to take stock of your progress. The original meaning of a benchmark was a geodesic brass marker (cadastral point) affixed to some rock marking a land surveyor's boundary. The result represents best practices and performances for similar activities, inside or outside an organization's industry. Organizations engage in benchmarking to understand the current point of a world-class performance. It could signify the location of a metric that measures how long processes take to complete that series or how many steps it took for completion.

However, comparison may be with peer and like industries and benchmarking conducted for similar categories with other industries to achieve world-class competitive comparison. As the saying goes, "insanity is doing the same thing over and over and expecting different results." Normally, benchmarking should be conducted outside the boundaries of like industries and with world-class organizations. The use of benchmarking creates a sense of urgency to find a compelling reason to change and to find new ways to continuously improve processes to conduct (rapid continuous improvements or rapid response time). Competitive or best-in-class benchmarking can create a sense of urgency as well as demonstrate the value of looking outside for ideas and comparisons.

Comparative benchmarking is establishing where an organization is with respect to industries like itself, and benchmarking for world-class competition is with those that have similar processes, as well as those that are not similar. External benchmarking helps to avoid setting the bar too low. Measuring one's own to other organizations, especially competitors, helps to keep the people in the organization focused on the market. This comparison is one of the first levels to gaining a competitive edge. To be outstanding, an organization must go beyond comparative benchmarking measurements.

Every organization must benchmark its data both internally and externally to assure progress is being made. Generally three years of data will provide a trend and five years of data will give better trends to ascertain information to make better-informed decisions.

Best practices are found in your own processes as well as in external processes. To reduce costs, increase revenues, and speed delivery as well as to increase customer satisfaction (the first platform from good to great for every organization), companies must begin to take advantage of the tremendous untapped talents and the reservoirs of knowledge in their organizations and to gather and apply benchmark data to their processes. Sometimes the best practices are referred to as *internal benchmarking* or *knowledge management.*

There are five types of benchmarking practices:

1. *Internal*—comparing one particular operation within one's organization with another; internal benchmarking is easy to implement.
2. *Competitive*—comparing an operation with direct competition like peer institutions and those in the same industry.

3. *Quantitative*—comparing productivity with any world-class operation; adapting one's own organization processes to that of a leading-edge organization (thinking out of the box), using quantitative measurements of both similar and different processes.
4. *Functional*—comparing an operation with that of a similar one within the broad range of an industry.
5. *Generic*—comparing operations from unrelated industries is the best form of seeking world-class operatives as compared to one's own.

Benchmarking is not the same as comparative studies that merely identify averages. Benchmarking must be closely linked with organizational value propositions, core values, vision, mission, strategies, goals, objectives, tactics, and actions. Benchmarking helps to create an effective organization with operational excellence that leads to a high level of relationship building and ultimately translates to customer success.

Nine simple ways of determining benchmarking processes or performance are listed below. (I discovered them when I visited Perth, Western Australia, for the Association of Tertiary Education Management system conference as the representative of Iowa State University and the Association of Higher Education Facilities Officers (APPA) as the 2005 APPA president-elect.)

The benchmarking process used by Swinburne University of Technology, Australia, as described by Fiona Clark, planning and quality officer, is a simple methodology that anyone can emulate:

1. Examine your processes and required performance.
2. Determine what needs to be improved and what needs to be benchmarked.
3. Find partners with which to benchmark, like those organizations who have best practices that are relevant to the area in which you are interested or are practical for benchmarking, e.g., confidentiality requirements.

4. Analyze their successful processes and performances as they pertain to your own experiences and develop key performance indicators.
5. Compare your performance with what you have analyzed with partners or other world-class operatives.
6. Identify your own strengths, weaknesses, opportunities, and threats and determine what gaps exist in your processes.
7. Develop options and plans for improvements.
8. Implement changes and improvements to close the gaps.
9. Review performances and further opportunities for continuous quality improvement.

Make sure you take before and after photographs that are applicable for recording the current reality for planning to reach the future-state conditions or to attain the ideal-state conditions. Remember that a picture is worth a thousand words.

To fill gaps through gap analysis, an organization must benchmark itself with its competition. Benchmarking establishes a place for setting performance standards that represent the outcomes or results of an organization's best possible practices and then tracking progress by measuring at regular intervals. Benchmarking helps in reducing the gap between the "actual" and the "desired" performance. To be outstanding, an organization must go beyond comparative benchmarking measurements and look for world-class metrics.

Benchmarking helps to create an effective organization with operational excellence that leads to a high level of relationship building and which ultimately translates to customer success. When an organization aligns itself and achieves self-equity and organizational equity concurrently, then key performance indicator measures must be put in place, i.e., "dashboards to success."

KNOWLEDGE MANAGEMENT

It became more evident as we continued on our 12-year quality journey that I needed an individual to focus on gathering and disseminating our data internally and externally to share our fact-based, data-driven, data-informed, and knowledge-based information. In 2000, I created a knowledge management position in our organization. Knowledge management is finding the right information for the right people in the organization at the right time. It is the conscious strategy of putting both tacit and explicit knowledge into action by creating a context infrastructure that enables people in an organization to use the collective data, taxonomy, and information as knowledge for the benefit of the entire enterprise. Access to knowledge is important in an operation, but access to people with knowledge is more important. No matter what an organization does to inculcate knowledge management and no matter what the reasons are for establishing a knowledge management work unit, *it is important that the right people get the right knowledge at the right time.*

A knowledge management focus for an organization is the next logical step to garner all the intellectual capital and institutional memory that resides in an organization and requires data mining of pertinent information for appropriate actions. To have your arms around the intellectual capital of the organization is, in essence, the creation of a knowledge management operative for ultimate organizational alignment. Alignment is the precursor to a mechanism leading to an effective organization banded by a group of highly skilled teams that function seamlessly for the good of the enterprise in a common cause. There are 10 basic categories of knowledge management:

1. Customer-focused knowledge
2. Transfer of knowledge and best practices
3. Intellectual asset knowledge management
4. Personal knowledge
5. Community of practice knowledge
6. Learning communities knowledge
7. Universal repository of knowledge
8. Knowledge management as a business strategy

9. Innovation and knowledge creation
10. Knowledge discovery

KNOWLEDGE CAPITAL

All enterprises compete based on knowledge capital. It is that profound knowledge in business, operation, and process levels of an organization added to the skills and experience of the knowledge-based workers that enables each organization to better serve its customers. Knowledge capital is important to improve businesses operations and processes and to speed delivery of goods, products, and services to market. The quest to be the first to market is sometimes a life-and-death situation. Nearly all organizations (from churches and armies to businesses and charities) depend on knowledge to flourish; knowledge capital is needed nearly everywhere. To fulfill this critical need there must be champions and teams of individuals dedicated to the support of the art and science of this technology. The *Baldrige Scorebook* uses the term "knowledge assets."

KNOWLEDGE ASSETS

Knowledge assets refers to the accumulated intellectual resources of your organization.[5] It is the knowledge possessed by your organization and its workforce in the form of information, ideas, learning, understanding, memory, insights, cognitive and technical skills, and capabilities. Your workforce, software, patterns, databases, and documents are repositories of your organization's knowledge assets. Knowledge assets reside not only within an organization but within its customers, suppliers, and partners as well.

Knowledge assets are the know-how that your organization has available to use, to invest, and to grow. Building and managing its knowledge assets are key components for your organization to create value for your stakeholders and to help sustain a competitive advantage. As Dov Seidman says in his book *How: Why How to Do*

Anything Means Everything ... in Business and in Life (John Wiley, 2007), it is not what a company does but how it does its business that will be the factor in the future.

ALIGNMENT

Alignment of an organization's departments for cross-functional operatives is the cornerstone for setting up parameters leading to strategic planning, which is the most important milestone in the quest to become the best. Alignment of organizations can be achieved by putting into place practices that promote self-equity and subsequently organizational equity, with the implementation of measurable high-performance expectations and reliable process improvements, using various classic quality tools, including tools that may be developed in the future. This is about increasing the number of pioneers from the "settlers" who later become "transformers" in the organization, and it is about coping with the CAVE people (citizens against virtually everything). Unless you map your processes, it is difficult to know where you are in the current reality—the "is" condition. Each organization must determine what it does by mapping each of its activities to get a better understanding of what to align.

The term *alignment* refers to consistency of plans, processes, information, resource decisions, actions, results, and analyses to support key organization-wide goals. Effective alignment requires a common understanding of purposes and goals. It also requires the use of complementary measures and information for planning, tracking, analyzing, and improving at three levels: (1) the organizational level, (2) the key process level, and (3) the work unit level (MBNQA 2007).[6]

ALIGNMENT AND ORGANIZATIONAL COMMITMENT

Cross-functional aligning assures that an organization's structure, systems, and operational processes all contribute toward creating the vision and mission such that it meets and exceeds customer expectations. The relationship between organizational alignment and commitment gives the probability of a "breakthrough" change. When alignment is highest, the probability of behavior modification and change has the greatest chance of success. Conversely, when alignment suffers and morale is low, change is trivialized and insignificant. The successive progression of sigmoid curves is presented to show the generations of pathfinding, moving through the trough of chaos and then through the four stages of denial, resistance, acceptance, and commitment. Once out of these doldrums, the organization is poised to become a learning and teaching organization. Individuals of the organization will then be able to raise the bar from the as-is condition and move the organization to a high-performance status. (For the various steps, conditions, paradigms, and zones of influence see Figure 7.2.)

Alignment of an Organization Using Baldrige (Criteria for Organization Design)

Unless an organization is uniquely qualified to deal with its customers by understanding its own strengths and weakness, it will be unable to understand what is required to move from the current paradigm of doing business. In the 1980s when Japanese goods, products, and services proliferated in the U.S. market, Japan appeared to be an unstoppable competitive threat in the world arena. The Malcolm Baldrige criteria are responsible for boosting U.S. companies to become world-class enterprises.

Alignment of the Organization through Metrics, Using the Balanced Scorecard Plus

Performance measurement for organizations relies upon measures taken at the level of their work processes. The implication for performance measurement is that the information needs, as expressed by the Balanced Scorecard dimensions, are addressed via measures collected because of executing the organization's work processes. Therefore, the challenge is to:

1. Identify those points in the work processes where the "right data" are produced.
2. Develop procedures for "rolling up" the data to represent performance from an organizational perspective.

These challenges require detailed understanding of how the organization does its work, including the variations that occur on the data in the Balanced Scorecards. By developing a Balanced Scorecard that truly tells the story of your strategy, you will set the foundation for a management system that is capable of driving dramatic improvements in performance through appropriate "metrics." The Balanced Scorecard was designed to measure organizational performance. One of its key strengths is the monitoring of several dimensions of performance of an organization.

Alignment of the Organization through Measurement

The challenge today is increasingly concerned with performance in five themes that are key to successful performance measurement:

1. A multidimensional view of performance.
2. Alignment of the measurement process through the layers of the organization.
3. Integration of performance measurement with a performance management system that is deployed systematically throughout the organization.
4. Identifying those points in the work processes where the right data are produced.
5. Developing procedures for "rolling up" the data to represent performance from an organizational perspective.

These themes require detailed understanding of how the organization does its work as well as the variations that occur on the data in the Balanced Scorecards.

Alignment of the Organization through Process Management

Process management is one opportunity that brings to the forefront a vehicle for managing changes and facilitating change in facilities operations. In these turbulent times, change is inevitable—whether it is in our personal life or in a quality journey to improve an organization's processes. It is inescapable that in both circumstances, change will come with time. We are at a point in the history of organizational changes where we have no choice but to move swiftly with agility. To be competitive, we must use all the skills, expertise, experience, and methodologies at our disposal. Knowledge-based workers will have the necessary skill sets to initiate actions and to motivate themselves by managing things and leading others in a learning and teaching organization.

Alignment of the Organization Using Lean and Six Sigma Methodologies

In the area of process management, which will be explained in more detail in a later chapter, there are two quality tools that will help to fill the gaps identified in the system model: Lean and Six Sigma.

Lean

1. Eliminates waste (*muda*) through continuous improvement of currently established processes.
2. Maximizes value-stream mapping with the intent of eliminating and/or minimizing non-value-added operations.
3. Eliminates searching, walking, and waiting.

Six Sigma

1. Eliminates defects associated with variation.
2. Optimizes processes to exceed customer expectations.

3. Focuses on financial results with laserlike intensity.
4. Measures errors in parts per million.
5. Provides breakthrough improvements (quantum).

Integrated Lean and Six Sigma methodologies, called the *the Lean Sigma Way* here, create high performance in process improvements where process capabilities are measured using statistics, common science, and complex science opportunities for defining, measuring, analyzing, improving, and controlling processes for alignment.

Alignment of the Organization Using Other Quality Tools

Quality tools have been in existence for many decades, from the days of Hammurabi in Babylonia to the scientific measurement theories propounded by Frederick Winslow Taylor in 1881. Frederick Taylor is by far the most influential theorist of modern times. He had an impact on management philosophy and practice. Since Frederick Taylor, many quality proponents have focused on one single quality tool. In bringing about process improvement, only a few have spoken about the harmony among the use of the many quality tools available to the practitioner. Using the right tools to achieve the end goal and arriving at the pinnacle of success is the quest to become the best.

Many enterprises are now using appropriate quality tools or a combination of tools to achieve their end goals. As the old saying goes, "any road will lead you there" if you have the time to wait for things to happen, but time is of the essence for any enterprise aspiring to reach the top quickly. An old Chinese adage says appropriately, "A man must sit in a chair with his mouth open for a very long time before a roast duck will fly in." No individual or organization can wait forever for things to happen and must therefore move with a sense of urgency. Without the aid of a burning platform as a catalyst, it may be difficult to budge your organization to move forward.[7]

Alignment of the Organization through High-Level Relationship Building

Good customer relationship skills add to individual and organizational equity since these skills deal with crucial conversations, and crucial confrontations with the customer. As the authors of the best-seller *Crucial Confrontations* say, "Companies that make impressive improvement in key performance areas (and eventually master them) are generally no different than others in their efforts to improve." However, when something is wrong, "people step up, speak up."[8] "The quality of your life depends on the quality of your communications," says Tony Robbins, a very popular motivational speaker and coach.

The rewards for developing effective relationships include long-term promotion of business, mutually satisfying relationships, repeat business for the organization, loyalty of the customer to the vendor, and acceptance of the brand of the product or services.

ALIGNMENT FOR CUSTOMER SUCCESS

Customer success is a "one plus more" mantra—a paradigm going beyond "customer delight." It is exceeding expectations and customer satisfaction, which is arriving at the "moment of truth." Customer satisfaction is fulfilling customers' expectations, and the "moment of magic" is like knowing what it takes to get to customer delight. If an organization merely focuses on customer service, it is only looking at short-term gains. The vendor determines customer service and the customer determines customer satisfaction. The vendor and customer both determine customer success in a mutually interdependent relationship based on paradigms, which are discussed in Chapter 7. However, much of the customer success alignment depends on building self-equity and organizational equity in your organization.

Once an organization has achieved self-equity and organizational equity concurrently, then key performance indicator measures must be put in place—dashboards to success (see Chapter 9).

These measures provide the appropriate metrics for determining the critical success factors for any business enterprise. To develop appropriate metrics, an organization must have knowledge workers who are well equipped to stand in two worlds simultaneously—one foot in current reality, with mastery of profound knowledge of processes and operatives, and the other foot in the future or ideal state, a world of tomorrow where things should be better than the current reality state. In this realm of things the organization is now poised and ready to move to world-class stature, from good to great, the ideal state—starting from the bottom line of world class, which is the could-be condition.

ALIGNMENT FOR CUSTOMER SUCCESS
THROUGH PARTNERING FOR PROFITS

There are three key areas of organizational alignment necessary for successful alliances to proceed toward profitability.[9] They are:

1. Strategic Fit
2. Cultural Fit
3. Operational Fit

Alliance deliverables become, better, cheaper, and faster only when the above three key areas have a reasonable alignment among the various organizations entering into a strategic alliance. To be successful, a strategic alliance involves making sure that partnerships fit in the above three areas. This dynamic applies regardless of the size of the partners involved—small businesses to global organizations. When selecting partners for future alliances, be sure to view the pros and cons through the three areas needed for alignment fit. This is especially true for multinational corporations.

SELF-ASSESSMENT

In both a public and a private enterprise, it is considered wise for organizational units to go through periodic reviews. Periodic reviews conducted throughout the organization enable cross-functional alignments and reveal misalignments to be corrected or prevented. Typically, the motivations for such reviews include the following:

1. Resource allocations
2. Planning
3. Restructuring or reengineering of operations
4. Reorganizations
5. Feedback reports, such as "Opportunities for Improvements" through Baldrige criteria reviews and evaluations at the state and national levels

These motivations are essentially driven by questions concerning quality and scope of programs and services provided vis-à-vis resources utilized; unmet needs; underserved clients; demonstrable, organizational, effectiveness; and operational excellence through efficiencies.

A self-assessment is an exercise normally done in a university setting to find out if it meets accreditation requirements or to check the pulse of the institution. In a private enterprise organization, self-assessments are conducted for CEO perception checks of the business units. Generally, an organization checks itself on how well it provides goods, products, and services, or some combination thereof.

A Baldrige application is a self-assessment tool that provides such an assessment through a formal description of how each organization operates. The examining bodies review the application to determine if the organization is meeting the criteria requirements in each of seven categories in order to receive an award and recognition of its prowess. The assessment of a unit's contributions to the overall mission and strategic plan of the enterprise is central to the review process. Most importantly, comprehensive reviews provide the impetus for future planning and appropriate changes involving strategies that are systematic, thoughtful, and long-ranged.

SETTING THE STAGE FOR STRATEGIC PLANNING

As Stephen Covey, author of the book *Seven Habits of Effective People*, says, "Begin with the end in mind." When embarking on a quality journey, it's important to begin with the end in mind with a truly clear vision of your journey to become the best. At FP&M, we raised our aspiration to become world class and sought excellence in providing service for our institution through continuous improvement and process management operatives built on fact-based, data-driven, data-informed operatives.

THE NEW ENVIRONMENTAL IMPACTS

The strategic development of enterprises as we know them today is being affected as a consequence of meeting these new challenges. Rather than the annual senior leadership meeting or having a team process at the strategic planning process (which traditionally happened once every three to five years), the enterprise has relegated responsibilities to a more continual process on an ongoing basis as needed at the incremental level of development for all parts of its organization. Documented exercises from strategic planning activities now have a quicker turnaround time. A quarterly review for organization performance and expectations is more the norm than the exception. Organization strategic planning refinements are conducted now for current, for near, for short-term and for long-term outcomes with the need to keep the pulse of the organization in concurrence with current, near-term, and future requirements.

Organizations, to be oriented and agile, must be constantly positioning themselves to meet or exceed market conditions and globalization impacts. Strategic and tactical executions are closely linked, following each other closer and more frequently than in the past. Successful strategic and tactical execution is dependent upon a clear vision of the future, an articulated rendition of strategies, objectives, and action plans that lead to an effective decision-making process with input from the senior and middle-level management—all conducted quickly and simultaneously. Organizational conflict and clear misalignments will occur if these two groups do not work well together across functional boundaries. Issues may not be aligned if all segments of the organization are not in synch. Cultural lag and reduction in time for process optimization are important aspects to organizational effectiveness and operational excellence.

Since most executives of corporations are receiving pressure from a multitude of stakeholders to rapidly deliver new and better results, cultural change in organizations is a difficult row to hoe. In many organizations there is a conflict between what is easy to do and what is the right or strategic or tactical thing to do in the best interests of the enterprise. When the leadership team chooses to do what is easy, rather than what is strategic, tactical, and appropriate for the situation, there are bound to be organizational design problems. The harder and more complex strategic and tactical change initiatives become lost. The impacts of globalization for current, near-term, short-term, and long-term situations demand more scrutiny and careful management of limited resources.

Larry Bossidy, the retired CEO of Honeywell who coauthored *Execution: The Discipline of Getting Things Done* (Crown Business, 2002), notes that "thinking does not matter if nothing happens." While there is significant value in taking the time to reflect, think, and review, the goal of strategic planning is better strategic execution.

Each organization's leadership team must have the discipline and perspective to understand how to execute at the strategic and tactical levels. Although the mantra today is "doing more with less," it appears that few are creating an infrastructure for proper execution after building fact-based, data-driven, data-informed, and knowledge-based operatives. Just focusing on getting people to do more or doing more with less may not be the answer for an organization seeking high performance levels. The "24/7" obsessive-compulsive behavioral pattern of the overachiever is now the norm. Now, everyone is expected to "put the pedal to the metal," working harder and longer for innovative and creative ideas and operatives to beat the competition in the continuing mantra of better, cheaper, faster.

QUALITY IMPROVEMENTS

Quality improvement principles are key to the success of any strategic planning process, and effective outcomes are a result of proper attention to input—people, machines, material, methods, and environment—with proper attention to how an organization treats its customers and work processes.

STRATEGIC PLANNING: THE BASICS

Planning is a fundamental principle of good business. We all know the importance of good planning. But how effective are most of our efforts? And how often are our plans actually implemented? Answers can be ferreted out through these objectives:

1. Understand the benefits of strategic planning.
2. Understand the five products of strategic planning.
3. Learn the three keys to successful planning and implementation.

With the best intentions, many organizations still spend most of their time reacting to unexpected changes in the environment instead of anticipating and preparing for them. This approach is sometimes called crisis management response. Because we are so often caught off guard, we may spend a great deal of time and energy "playing catch-up." And because we often expend so much energy coping with immediate problems, there seems to be little energy left to take a look ahead, anticipate, and prepare for the next challenges before they are upon us. This can become a vicious cycle that locks many organizations into a reactive posture.

However, it doesn't have to be that way. A well-tested process called *strategic planning* provides a viable alternative to crisis management. Strategic planning is the cornerstone of organizational development for successful outcomes. This is the second criterion in the seven management systems for organizational management and the road map to becoming competitive for future-oriented, organizational growth.

Strategic planning is a step-by-step process with definite objectives and end products that can be implemented and evaluated. Very simply, it is a process by which we look into the future and paint a picture of that future based on current trends and the forces that will affect and influence us. Unlike most long-range planning that looks ahead one year at most, strategic planning looks three to five years ahead and charts a definite course based on strong indicators of what the business environment will be like in those years.

These indicators include census demographic statistics, economic indicators, government policies, and technological advances. They reveal strong trends regarding changes in lifestyles and economic and political climates, which are important factors. Some of these trends are potential opportunities, some are potential threats, and some are both. But clearly examining the very real possibilities and formulating strategies to meet the challenges can help the organization take full advantage of opportunities and minimize threats. In short, we can take control of the future. We can use our energies and resources more effectively, which will enable us to conduct business more successfully despite changes in the environment.

WHY STRATEGIC PLANNING?

Besides the personal satisfaction of taking charge of the organization's future, there are at least five compelling reasons for using strategic planning:

1. It forces us to look into the future and, therefore, provides an opportunity to influence the future, or at least assume a proactive posture.
2. It provides better awareness of our needs and those of the facilities-related issues and of the environment.

3. It helps define the overall mission of the organization and focuses on the objectives.
4. It provides a sense of direction, continuity, and effective staffing and leadership.
5. It plugs everyone into the system and provides standards of accountability for people, programs, and allocated resources.

In summary, strategic planning is the key to helping us, collectively and cooperatively, to gain control of the future and the destiny of our organizations. The overall goal of strategic planning is to produce a plan that can be successfully implemented. Along the way, the following seven products of strategic planning will be developed, evaluated, and refined:

1. Environmental issues and trends
2. Needs survey
3. Mission statement
4. General objectives
5. Strategies
6. Action plans
7. Tactical plans

KEYS TO SUCCESSFUL STRATEGIC PLANNING AND IMPLEMENTATION

Suppose your organization thoroughly develops all seven products of strategic planning, completes the process, and comes up with a strategic plan. Everyone has the best of intentions, but when we get back to our units, we are overwhelmed with daily details. Pretty soon it's back to "business as usual." The plan sits on the shelf, and before we know it, another year has passed. This need not happen! There are three major keys to successful strategic planning and implementation:

• Commitment
• Credibility
• Communication

First, let's consider commitment. We're talking about commitment up front by the leadership of our units. Commitment means no shortcuts. Shortcuts undermine the validity of the results, so commitment must include an adherence to the full and thorough process of strategic planning. There must also be a *commitment to implementing* the strategies recommended by the strategic planning committee.

The leaders should implement programs and services and commit allocations to meet the objectives of the strategic plan at a level that is "doable" or feasible for your particular organization and level of activity. To put it very succinctly, to commit to plan is to commit to change.

The second key to implementation is credibility. Credibility is created and maintained by following three guidelines:

1. Representative participation
2. Adherence to the complete process
3. Clear documentation

The strategic planning committee should keep clear documentation of all its research and activities. This documentation will serve two purposes: (1) it will serve as the basis for the strategic plan and its background materials; (2) it will serve as a clear record of the committee's activities open for all to see and evaluate. There should be nothing exclusive or secret about strategic planning. It should be open (transparent) to all for review and input.

This leads us to the key to successful implementation: communicate findings at every point. It is important to explain the principles and goals of strategic planning to all units. We need to assure each person that even though he or she may not be on the committee, everyone is a "de facto member" and can have input and evaluate the recommendations. It will be up to the staff and committees to determine how to fulfill each objective. The strategic planning committee recommends in general *what* they think should be done. The leadership, operating committees, and staff determine *how* it will be done. Strategic planning is the key to assuring that the organization is prepared for the challenges of tomorrow.

DESIGNING HOW TO GET THERE

Chapter 3 describes the level of changes needed. Figure 3.2 shows the level of changes and what the organization needs to go through in order to move from level one changes to level five outcomes and beyond for greater than Six Sigma results. One of the premises of designing how to get there is to understand the definition of design. The definition of design is that it is an exercise into the unknown with expectations of a predetermined set of outcomes relevant to an identified problem. Design in this sense is something that is not usually done. Therefore, it requires the expertise of the organization's intellectual capital to determine the outcome through a process of designing how to get there. Design and develop new solutions by asking new and better questions, by letting go of some predetermined solutions derived from the existing organizational culture, by looking at a new structure, and by doing a paradigm shift.

HOW LONG WILL IT TAKE?

For an organization to grow and prosper, it must train and develop its people to meet current and future challenges. Depending on the current stage of development, this can be a challenging effort. Building the appropriate foundation is a sequential proposition one step at a time. There are no quick fixes to make major behavioral changes. The first stage (see Figure 2.3) involves recognizing the problems and issues by identifying and putting in writing where the organization stands; the second stage involves identifying, clarifying, and agreeing on the attainable goals; the third stage involves listing the problems and issues and defining, measuring, and analyzing the processes required to attain the goals. Portions of stages three and four may overlap and run concurrently to obtain "quick wins." During these two stages the processes are improved, piloted, and implemented. Portions of stage four may overlap stage five, where processes will be controlled, standardized, and readied for integration of continuous quality improvements into stage five.

Most organizations take a minimum of three to seven years to get started. This is described as one cycle of development in Chapter 5. In my opinion a starter organization must go through three cycles from the current condition, to should-be, to the ideal state. It takes three cycles for maturation of an organization.

Sister Mary Jean Ryan, CEO of SSM Healthcare in St Louis, which was the first national healthcare recipient of the national Malcolm Baldrige Quality Award, stated that it took them 21 years to achieve the award. SSM used the state programs to get started and then, after they won the national, encouraged all of their member hospitals to use their state programs to continue the improvement.

WHAT IS A VALUES-BASED ORGANIZATION?

The task of creating a values-based organization to achieve world-class stature is not readily accepted and is beyond the comfort zone of many individuals in an organization. Most folks have been used to dwelling in the certainty arena, and to break this pattern requires a lot of work and cultural and behavioral change. The changes we made in our operations moved individuals in the organization out of their comfort zone from certainty to uncertainty, requiring them to develop a mastery of skills and knowledge in the areas of their focus. The seven critical "masteries" are described in Chapter 5 and listed below:

1. Business model mastery
2. Customer focus solutions mastery
3. Supply chain mastery
4. Process mastery
5. Integration and data mastery

6. Human resource mastery
7. Innovation and differentiation mastery

INTEGRATION

Integration is expected to occur in a mature organization where all the processes are aligned and the right conditions for an effective organization with operational excellence are provided. Baldrige criteria 2007, "Criteria for Performance Excellence," outlines steps toward a mature process beginning with:

- Reacting to problems
- Early systematic approaches
- Alignment approaches
- Integrated approaches

Reacting to problems are operations characterized by activities, rather than by processes, and they are largely responsive to immediate needs or problems rather than long-term goals. At this stage of an operation the goals are poorly defined.

Early systematic approaches to operations show the beginning stages of conducting operations by processes with repeatability, evaluation, and improvement, and some early coordination among organizational business units. At this stage strategy and quantity goals are being defined.

Alignment approaches operations are characterized by processes that are repeatable and regularly evaluated for improvement, with shared learning and coordination among organizational units. At this stage the processes address key strategies and goals of the organization.

Integrated approaches operations are characterized by processes that are repeatable and regularly evaluated for change and improvement in collaboration with other affected units. Efficiencies across units are sought and achieved through analysis, innovation, and the sharing of information and knowledge. At this stage of the operation, the processes and measures are tracked for progress on key strategic and operational goals.

REACHING THE IDEAL STATE OF A WORLD-CLASS ORGANIZATION

How do you know when you have reached world-class stature is a question with which most organizations will be faced. Each organization is unique and the methodology by which it attains this level of high performance operation depends on how it takes the journey to reach the goal. (See Chapter 5.) The struggle for each organization is then to constantly maintain and sustain world-class practices.

World-class organizations are customer focused (satisfaction, delight, and success) on doing the right things rather than on doing things right. Internal customers are treated with the same reverence and care as external customers. The focus is on core values in a values-based organization, understanding the core competencies and core business propositions. As each business unit functions, business units operate expertly with mastery. There will be service-level agreements among internal work groups to help assure optimum productivity at the least cost, in other words, better, cheaper, faster. Therefore, a question must be asked: Who are the stakeholders? The stakeholders are the voice of the customers and the voice of the employees (see Chapter 6).

Additionally, the following questions must be posed about the stakeholder groups:

1. What are the communication objectives?
2. What is their background?
3. What mechanism should be used to engage them?
4. What type of information should be developed for consumption?
5. What is the format?

6. What is the frequency of communication?
7. What kind of reporting and measures must be received?

The answers take the operations to the next level of excellence.

NOTES

1. http://en.wikipedia.org/wiki/Cecilia_Payne-Gaposchkin#Quotation.
2. Peter W. Keen, *The Process Edge: Creating Values Where It Counts*, Harvard Business School Press, 1997.
3. Harry Mikel and Richard Schroder, *Six Sigma*, Doubleday, 2000.
4. H. J. Harrington, *Business Process Improvement: The Breakthrough Strategy for Total Quality, Productivity, and Competitiveness*, McGraw-Hill, 1991.
5. http://www.baldrige.nist.gov/Business_Criteria.htm, page 68.
6. http://www.baldrige.nist.gov/Business_Criteria.htm, page 65.
7. Christopher K. Ahoy, "Leadership in Educational Facilities Administration," APPA 2007, Alexandria, VA, page 82.
8. Kerry Patterson, Joseph Grenny, Ron McMillan, and Al Switzler, *Crucial Confrontations*, McGraw-Hill, New York, 2005.
9. http://www.businessvideos.tv/collaboration/?surveyCode=2712&keyCode=156 095_4.

Creating a World-Class Organization

> *"The roots of true achievement lie in the will to become the best that you can become."*
>
> Harold Taylor[1]

DEFINING *WORLD CLASS*

A world-class organization produces goods or services with unbiased repeatable consistency—better, cheaper, and faster than its competition. An organization that is outstanding in every aspect of its performance is world class. Being world class is going beyond excellence to become great! If you have ever watched Olympic summer or winter games, you will find world-class athletes excelling in all areas of their endeavors to become the best. World class connotes that experience of being the best of the best.

When 99.4 percent of operations are identified as being average, it means:

1. One hour of unsafe drinking water every month
2. No electricity for almost 90 hours each year
3. Two unsafe plane landings each day at Chicago O'Hare airport
4. 16,000 pieces of lost mail, mishandled by the U.S. Postal Service each hour

5. 500 incorrect surgical operations each week
6. 50 newborn babies lost each day
7. 32,000 missed heartbeats per person each year
8. 12 babies given to the wrong parents each day
9. 22,000 checks debited from the wrong account each hour
10. 5,520,000 cases of soft drinks produced flatter than a bad tire each year

Average means 99.4 percent capability or 3σ – 67,210 defects per million opportunities (DPMO) compared to 3.4 DPMO for world-class status. See Table 2.1.

> "We are what we repeatedly do. Excellence, therefore, is not an act, but a habit."
>
> Aristotle[2]

WHY ASPIRE TO BE WORLD CLASS?

One reason for organizations to aspire to become world class is the impact now being felt by globalization across our brave new world of the 21st century, where everything is moving exponentially faster. To understand the nuances of all that is taking place, and to absorb the impacts, we need to put in place an organization that is moving toward near perfection, moving toward a world-class

Average	World-Class
99.4% Error-free processes	99.9997% Error free processes
Approximately 6,810 products out of a million will not meet specifications	Three products out of a million will not meet specifications
Expect cold showers 54 hours per year	Expect cold showers two minutes per year
Electricity goes off one hour per week	Electricity goes off two seconds per week

Table 2.1 Average versus World Class

operational excellence. It is said that if you repeat something constantly, it soon becomes a behavior, which turns into a habit. A habit becomes your character, and soon it becomes your destiny. Hence, there is a reason to look at how human development has taken place to understand the importance of being world class.

When we look at the development of the human species through our historical development, we may draw some analogies for planning. To view mankind's development in phases and to learn lessons from each segment, we must check for what is embedded in each of the stages of the *Homo sapiens* organizational development progression and, perhaps, prepare ourselves to meet what lies ahead.

The Hindu scriptures, the *Bhagavad Gita*, many centuries ago predicted that we were moving from the *Kali Yuk* (the Sanskrit word meaning "flesh age") to the *Sataya Yuk* (the spiritual age of consciousness). Figure 2.1 shows the progression of organizational development and the human intellectual development progression from the days of the hunters to the present day and beyond to the spiritual age of consciousness.

Agrarian Age

In the agrarian age, brawn and physical labor were required to farm the land. The objective of the agrarian society was to have a lot of children, strong ones. The economic well-being of all depended on the availability of many hands to help with the chores. The expression "many hands make light work" is true. Those were hard times, life was harsh, and medicine was not easily available (not all would survive famine and pestilence). Those who would die at an early age from disease or other calamities needed to be replaced. So one of the reasons for having a large family was survival by the numbers—to fill the gaps. The paradigm of the agrarian society was to cultivate enough food to feed the members of the growing population.

Note that the entities within each era in Figure 2.1 had to determine what the "best of the best" meant—how this determination

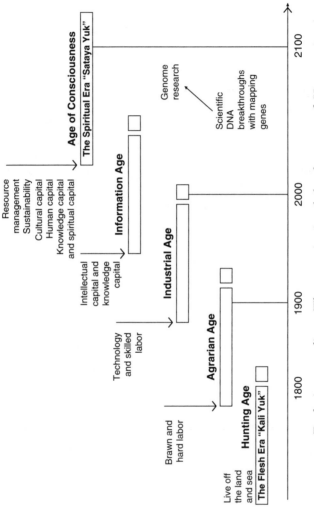

Figure 2.1 Evolution paradigm. The organizational development of *Homo sapiens* is a journey from the flesh era (Kali Yuk) to the spiritual era (Sataya Yuk).

would be part of their psyche, and how one became differentiated from others for survival.

Industrial Age

When James Watt invented the steam engine, smokestacks in England became the symbol of the advent of the industrial revolution. To populate their factories, industries were looking for workers able to understand and use technology and skills. To fill this need, farm hands moved from the fields to factories, resulting in fewer and fewer people on the family farms. People were trained for assembly line product manufacturing. The new technology required skilled labor to operate machines that needed care and nurturing and manipulation. Machines produced products at a prolific pace, and mass production was the norm.

This was the era that most of our parents or grandparents enjoyed—a lifetime of employment in one company, that is, until robotics began producing things better, cheaper, and faster than human hands. Change is inevitable, and change is an ordeal for many employees, but if you want your organization to succeed, you must change and adapt to new technologies. It cannot be avoided. You will be assimilated.

Information Age

When automobiles and trains arrived, they were 10 times (an order of magnitude) the speed of man and horse. This caused an industrial revolution. Then cars, trains, and airplanes arrived at an order of magnitude even faster, resulting in another industrial revolution. Then came rockets at 25,000 mph, still another order of magnitude faster and another industrial revolution. Supercomputers arrived around 1965, but they are not an order of magnitude faster; they are many millions of times faster, and we have no idea how this will manifest!

At the same time, the Control Data Corporation's 6600 supercomputer arrived with its 60-bit word that comprised a 48-bit mantissa and a 12-bit characteristic. And, at 15 million operations per second, it could keep up with everyone in the world multiplying by hand. Today, your home desktop computer, with a 2.4 GHz processor, can do that. Just try to imagine the future with teraflop and petaflop speeds.

Age of Consciousness—Spiritual Age

We are now at the beginning of still another evolution, nanotechnology. Centuries after the age of the hunters and gatherers and after the age of agriculture, we are approaching the end of the industrial age. At least that is true in some sectors of the United States as factories go abroad to developing third world countries. The new future industries, cultivated by brainpower and machines that operate at the molecular level, are moving from the information age of intellectual capital and knowledge capital. We now see manifestations of the advent of the spiritual age. We will be creating spiritual workers, not bound by religious dogma, but bound by the grace of humanity with their consciousness levels.

We are moving toward the consciousness age where resource management, sustainability, cultural capital, human capital, intellectual capital, knowledge capital, and, finally, spiritual capital will play a major role in the makeup of the world in which we live and, hopefully, continue to breathe. Time is running out for our planet earth, and we must do what we can to preserve the good for the generations coming after us. It is the right thing to do. The only way we can do that is to inculcate into individuals and organizations the concept of world-class operatives. Mediocrity in our operations is not good enough!

Why not? Being mediocre is not an option for any organization that wishes to make a mark in this global economy where the world is "flat." Competition from all parts of the world will be the focus of any enterprise for the next 10 to 25 years. No country has a monopoly on brainpower. Creating a world-class operation is a must for any organization desiring to meet the challenges of globalization. The rest of the world is developing labor forces that are educated, capable, and perhaps equally well versed in most of the necessary concepts and techniques—concepts and techniques that can be execute at a much lower cost. If we are not prepared to meet these onslaughts with the skill sets of a world-class generation of "knowledge-based workers," then what we do here for a living will be done by somebody else—anywhere, anyplace, anytime.

DOING MORE WITH LESS

New technology allows us to collect and disseminate information quickly and to mine (data-mine) the prolific data available to us for an evidence-driven culture. To mitigate staff shortages, budget decrements, and revenue shortfalls, we leverage technology to "do more with less." The safe harbor and safe haven created for employees fosters an atmosphere of cooperation, allowing commitment, consistency, creativity, competency, credibility, collaboration, and a high level of communication to take place through shared values—personal, employee, and organizational (see Figure 2.2).

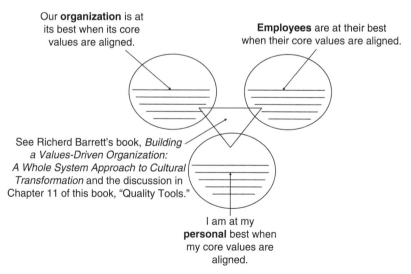

Person, Employee, Organization

Figure 2.2 Core values perspectives. The three circles of core values consist of the person, employees as a group, and the organization as a whole.

MOVING AN ORGANIZATION UP A NOTCH

The need to move an organization up a notch becomes evident as we begin to strive to meet the challenges of the 21st century. To bring these challenges to the forefront, we need to shift *from an organizational task focus to a process focus*. To detect and remove any bottlenecks or waste, we can no longer look at the organization through disjointed tasks, and we must scrutinize each and every process. Process connections and interdependencies and interrelatedness must be viewed from a systems approach, a holistic way of observing things.

To build self-equity and organizational equity, an organization may use the Malcolm Baldrige seven criteria of management systems for organization design and the Balanced Scorecard Plus to determine appropriate metrics for measuring what matters and to identify key performance indicators—those that are responsive to our critical success factors. Organizations will use Lean and Six Sigma methodologies for process improvements through common sense, common science, and complex science, as discussed further in Chapter 3.

However, using quality tools is not good enough! It is evident that any organization is only as good as the people in it. Putting people first is the crux of any successful endeavor. In order to change the culture of the organization to accept changes, an organization must create many training opportunities for people to excel. Since things change—life is full of change and reaching for perfection means a lot of change—organizations need to ensure that behavior patterns are continually watched and modified to fit organizational needs. Therefore, every chance an organization gets it must create awareness in its employees for the need of a learning and teaching environment, where each employee learns and then teaches other employees.

LEARNING AND TEACHING ENVIRONMENT

To inspire and motivate others internally in any organization, leaders must create a "learning and teaching environment."

Leaders, down the line, must also nurture a holistic approach, where systemic and humanistic concepts are in balance—sort of the yin and yang of the organizational management approach. To develop a learning and teaching organization, we must create an environment capable of developing knowledge-based workers—workers who have the necessary skill sets to motivate themselves and others (volunteer versus conscripted) and to respond directly to the customers' requirements of better, cheaper, and faster for goods, products, and services with fact-based, data-driven, and knowledge-based information.

In learning and teaching organizations, employees are knowledge-based workers who have attained the training, education, skill sets, experience, and knowledge of the organization. Units need to move from the "is" condition—the baseline of any organization's starting point or the minimum condition, which, if not achieved, really "pisses people off." This is the must-be zone paradigm, or the current reality. Learning and teaching organizations need to move to the should-be condition or the "more than better" zone paradigm (the future state) from the current condition in a continuous improvement mode. Organizations are reaching to the base of the "ideal state" (the could-be condition) or the customer satisfaction zone paradigm. Achieving higher-level performance is explained graphically in the diagram of raising the bar (see Figure 7.2, which shows the various platform levels that an organization must ascend by filling in the gaps). The platform of the ideal state is merely the threshold of a good organization. This threshold is also known as "arriving at the moment of truth" platform, where the standard operating procedures are reached or meet the specifications. In the quality world this platform terminology is also noted as meeting ISO 9000 (clarification and verification).

> *"Discovery consists of seeing what everyone else has seen and thinking what nobody has thought."*
>
> Albert von Szent-Györgyi

OPERATIONAL LEADERSHIP ACADEMY

In the world-class journey workers need a safe environment, first to survive and then to thrive in what they do for the organization. Creating a safe environment for knowledge workers, allowing employees to develop skills, and encouraging them to look at things in new, different, and better ways and to ask good questions (if you need a better answer, ask a better question) is a paradigm shift for many operations,.

Old habits are hard to break, and change is unsettling for all of us. Though the tendency is to succumb to "if it ain't broke, don't fix it," the competitive edge resolution is change it for the better. However, people need to be taught and educated, especially at the second-tier leadership—those who are coming up the pipeline of leadership through their own fortitude, discipline, and aspiration. For those who need to be uplifted with extra training, you need to create an online leadership academy with safety training as the primary target to develop people in your organization. Additionally, you should establish training sessions through an operational leadership academy and new employee orientation programs. Second-tier managers who have primary responsibilities for promoting operating excellence in their respective units in a supervisory or nonsupervisory position, and who hold important process owners' responsibilities for organizational effectiveness, should also be included in these classes. This must be done to encourage and spur staff to take a leadership position in the organization whenever slots open up through succession or accession planning. Later on, a more formalized process needs to be established, like a training and development group, to fulfill the needs for access to series concepts for career progression that supports accession and succession planning within the organization.

Employees then learn to clarify issues and problems and to promote ideas in the pursuit of excellence, sharing new ideas and engaging others among different service groups. Other groups within the private sector and in the higher education community eagerly will seek these key staff members for their aptitude and capabilities. Therefore, these learning and teaching sessions will:

- Build an organization that works as a team to develop camaraderie with high performance with a built-to-last commitment. Through their consistency, competency, creativity, credibility, collaboration, and quality, including anticipatory communication through shared values, employees develop a common language from a common body of knowledge and an understanding about concepts of management philosophies.
- Clarify the definitions of what an effective organization really is and what it means to have operational excellence in promoting world-class awareness.
- Share the strategic planning process at every level through various mechanisms.
- Promote through high-level anticipatory communications; promote interdepartmental, cross-functional, process management effectiveness relationships. With the express purpose of meeting critical-to-customer requirements and critical-to-customer satisfaction, solve problems together. This, in turn, leads to customer success.
- Engage in benchmarking, sharing the lessons learned with like-minded professionals.

WHAT IS A WORLD-CLASS OPERATION?

A world-class operation is an organization that becomes the best and sustains itself as the best in its particular field of endeavor. To retain world-class status,[3] an organization must move from the performance excellence phase to strategic process management excellence, which includes the ideal state of "good to great."

A world-class operation is also an enterprise that is driven by a customer-based focus (customer-oriented organization) in relentless pursuit of going beyond excellence to become outstanding. According to Drs. Sang Lee and Fred Luthans, some companies have managed to go beyond the learning organization stage to become world-class organizations. These enterprises are leaders in their fields of endeavor and sustain their competitiveness through continuous quality improvements. A fluid, flexible, agile, or virtual organization promotes a healthy value of empowering employees through a creative human resource management system, mindful of employee developmental needs to meet the rigorous demands of an ever-changing job situation.

"A world-class organization can be described as being the best in class or better than its competitors around the world, at least in several strategically important areas."[4] To achieve world-class stature, an organization must be a strategically focused organization. To derive strategy for an organization, one must look at the following 12 steps or phases of development:

1. Core values
2. Vision
3. Mission
4. Strategy
5. Objectives
6. Measures
7. Targets
8. Initiatives
9. Implementation plan
10. Action plans
11. Integration and execution
12. Feedback

To achieve greatness through outstanding results, organizations must look at the organization's core values from three perspectives:

- The individual perspective relative to the organization
- The employees of the organization's perspective relative to the organization
- The organization's perspective in becoming the best it can be

Figure 2.2 shows how the three perspectives coalesce, a process which is necessary to derive a common ground perspective that becomes the driver for organizational changes through the organization's core values perspective. Three circles of core values include personal, employees as a group, and the organization as a whole. The responses to the individual circle and collected thought emanating from these three areas will be the outcome for the organization's core value propositions.

Generally, world-class operations produce six-sigma (6σ) levels of goods, products, and services. This means an enterprise has 99.997 percent yield capability, 3.4 defects per million opportunities (DPMO), and less than 10 percent of goods or products are returned by the customer or recalled by the manufacturers for preventative and corrective action. Compare this to the average level, which is a three-sigma (3σ) level of goods, products, and services. This means that 93.9 percent yield, 66,807 DPMO, almost 20 to 30 percent of goods, products, or services produced are defective or returned. For example, if you bought a computer and it costs around $1,200, the company with an average operation would be spending 20 to 30 percent of its sales fixing it before selling the product to you. The noncompetitive organization produces one- or two-sigma (1–2σ) levels of goods, products, or services and is bound to be out of work and bankrupt soon. This means they have only a 50 percent yield with a high level of defective goods, products, or services in the range of 330,000 to 680,000 DPMO, and greater than 40 percent of their goods, products, or services require fixing before sales due to the cost of poor quality.

ANYWHERE, ANYPLACE, ANYTIME

Often when we inform our employees of the need for a world-class operation, we point to the probability that if we do not do what is needed to be done to create a "customer success" environment, there will be some entity out there that will be ready, willing, and able to take our place anywhere, anyplace, anytime. The message resonates with many who understand that if we do not shape up and take our organization's operatives "up a notch" by doing the right things, we could be outclassed by another group that would do our jobs better, cheaper, and faster. In other words, we could be outsourced. At the same time, we also remind ourselves that we cannot just live on our laurels, and no matter how good we think we are, there is always the danger of complacency and of being upstaged. In order to keep ourselves agile, flexible, and light-footed to meet new challenges, we must always be on the path of continuous quality improvement. To be at the leading edge, we must also be in a state of continuous and never-ending quality initiatives and improvements. The following examples may help to clarify my meaning.

Only one out of the 12 largest U.S. industrial firms that began about 100 years ago has survived as of January 1, 2005. Take a moment to review some of the companies that evolved in the 19th century. What happened?

1. The American Cotton Oil Company
2. American Steel
3. American Sugar Refining
4. Continental Tobacco
5. Federal Steel
6. General Electric
7. National Lead
8. People's Gas
9. Tennessee Coil
10. Lever
11. US Iron
12. United States Rubber

Only General Electric survived, which is why so many books are written about this company. No others made it through the 100 years intact. While GE is in the mode of continuous and never-ending quality initiatives and improvements, there is a danger in only focusing on this paradigm and not understanding or heeding the voice of the customer and the voice of the employee. Tomorrow's companies are waiting to outwit and outchallenge even those who have sustained their niche in the market.

Of the industries listed, most were natural resource dependent and perhaps too ethnocentrically focused to be able to change with the times and phases of the human development changes presented here. Now take a look at some of the newer industries from the latter part of the 20th century that are not natural resource oriented. Why are they so different from the earlier industrial era?

1. Biotechnology
2. Civilian aircraft technology
3. Computer software
4. Electronics
5. Genomics
6. Hardware
7. Microelectric
8. Nanotechnology
9. Telecommunications
10. Videoconferencing

Each of these industries is a brainpower industry of the information age, unlike the previous natural resource companies. Ask the questions, 'Can these new industries be located anywhere, anyplace, anytime?' Are the natural resource industries hampered by location of people, machines, materials, methods, and environment? Is the environment causing raw material– and transportation-based industries to be not as important as these newer industries?

ORGANIZATION DESIGN, METRICS, AND PROCESS IMPROVEMENTS

World-class organizations are in search of a competitive edge through combining principles of organization design to produce products and services of high quality, at least cost and fastest delivery for their customers. Most of the organizations of the future aspire to move from a paradigm of surviving to a thriving modus operandi. To reach the appropriate high-level customer focus (customer satisfaction, delight, or success), an organization competing with the best of the best, which are world-class operations, must have goods, products, and services that are innovative and different from its competition.

INNOVATION AND DIFFERENTIATION

In their book *'Why Not?'* Nalebuff and Ayres share that innovation is just waiting to happen. Many of these innovations are right in front of our noses, and when we ask "why not," things happen. Potential improvements are just waiting to happen once the mind is activated to look at potential solutions everywhere. For example, ask the following questions:

1. Why not have firms call you back rather than have you wait on hold?
2. Why not sell generic first-class postage stamps that remain valid when rates go up?
3. Why not design a fixed-rate mortgage that automatically refinances when interest rates fall?

> *"The whole of science is nothing more than a refinement of everyday thinking."*
> Albert Einstein

World-class enterprises must position themselves to become leading-edge entities by innovation and differentiation and uniqueness through creating an effective organization with operational excellence grounded in an evidence-driven culture. Why not create a fact-based, data-driven, data-informed, and knowledge-based organization using system-thinking principles along with a holistic approach using appropriate quality tools harmoniously embedded in tacit knowledge? In a later chapter I explain how tacit knowledge is a natural progression from explicit knowledge (see Figure 3.4 in the next chapter). As each organization seeks the competitive edge, one of the premises for producing quality goods, products, and services is to use the appropriate quality tools. To engage the organization to move toward becoming the best in class, raise the bar from current reality to the future state and on to the ideal state. There are many quality tools that an organization can use to achieve world-class status.

DEFINITIONS

World class is being best in class. It is the goal of many individuals and organizations. This aspiration is composed of two parts, namely:

1. Being competitive (with others and with self)
2. Attaining the leading edge by becoming the best in an area of interest or focus and then becoming first—just like an Olympic athlete

Competitive

Competition is the ingredient necessary for an organization seeking to produce goods, products, and services equal to or better than its competition for customer satisfaction. One needs to be competitive because customers seek to acquire goods, products, and services of better quality, cheaper cost, and without delay— better, cheaper, and faster.

Leading Edge

Leading edge has two parts: Individuals or organizations need to be the best and then to become first in their areas of interest or expertise. Being world class is the ability of an organization to replicate high-quality goods, products, and services at the least cost, with quicker delivery than its competitors and at the same time responding to the critical needs of the customer.

> *"Organizations are constantly on the alert to gain a competitive edge, using the many tools that have long been touted as a way to beat the competition. Yet despite the focus on innovative ways of making products and providing service, there remains one constant: Organizations that produce better quality products and services than their rivals beat the competition time and time again."*
> George Ekes, *The Six Sigma Revolution*

Competition is motivation for a viable organization in the 21st century. The motivation and passion indispensable to taking the organization up a notch requires that the organization and individuals within acknowledge the need to become world class. An organization needs to have the right attitude, process, and tools in place to become competitive in the marketplace. It is a difficult proposition to move an already good solid organization to the next level, but it is not insurmountable. An organization can become world class by being competitive and then becoming leading edge. In other words, an organization must become the best in what it does, and then it must become first in its field of endeavor. Despite the focus on innovative ways of making products and providing service, there remains one constant: Organizations that produce better-quality products and services than their rivals beat the competition time and time again. Here is a list of competitive attributes that have to be developed:

- Ability to create value for customer satisfaction (pull)
- Adaptability to changing environment
- Agility (quick to change)
- Ability to anticipate what is coming down the pike
- Capability to cope with tumultuous changes
- Capacity to handle anything, anywhere, anytime.
- Competencies of the individual and organization
- Collaboration and engagement with others

- Communication of the very highest level
- Cultural capital with diversity
- Differentiation, ability to separate from competition
- Green management (sustainable products and services friendly to earth)
- Innovation for new goods, products, and services
- Intellectual capital and institutional memory
- Invisible capabilities of leadership
- Leveraging technology
- Multiply best practices quickly
- Nurture talents and create a field of opportunities for their growth
- Resource management
- Sense of urgency
- Speed of delivery
- Unique skills, techniques, human resources

COMPETITIVE ADVANTAGE

The key to competitive advantage is to create organizational effectiveness and operational excellence in any enterprise. To do this is to proactively gauge customer perceptions and to aggressively act on the findings to create great relationships between the provider and the consumer. Provider techniques for satisfying customers do not have to be difficult; they just have to be personable, timely, and effective.

> *"Competitive advantage is ... positioning a business to maximize the value of its capabilities that distinguish it from competitors."*
> Michael E. Porter, *Competitive Advantage: Creating and Sustaining Superior Performance*[5]

In the quest for a competitive advantage, most highly successful organizations are aspiring to obtain a strategic process management environment at a time when current events are requiring them to move their operations up a notch. To those who are at the cross-roads of launching a quality journey, I offer this book as an incentive to carry on. I encourage those enterprises that are already achieving world-class stature to use any information in this book to enhance their competitive position. I am passionate about process improvements in your organization and its ability in meeting global challenges by looking into concepts for implementing process management and lean thinking principles for value stream mapping. I encourage organizations to implement training and development programs and practices to build employee self-equity and thereby enhance organizational equity. I encourage organizations to measure progress in order to determine whether "measuring what matters" is really the key "dashboard to success" for developing high-level performances. I urge firms to use Lean and Six Sigma methodologies to remove waste, mistake-proof processes, and remove defects. It can be done.

World-Class Competitiveness

To meet the demand for the new economy, an organization must develop its people, machines, material, methods, and environment to be in a position of world-class competitiveness. At ISU, we are only looking at an integrated methodology to reach world-class stature among many options available. Our methodology includes three main tools—Baldrige, Balanced Scorecard Plus, and the Lean Sigma Way. These tools are readily available to you to produce world-class goods, products, and services.

There are a number of different approaches that may provide a high level of customer satisfaction, and they produce generous profits for the organization and its stakeholders. The processes discussed here involve just one way to respond to challenges of globalization and competitiveness. Although a number of tool kits are readily available to the practitioner, you may wish to emulate the exact three tools that we used to achieve our successes. Tools that are discussed in this book can assist you in reducing *muda*

(Japanese for "waste"), in increasing productivity and in making a profit for your enterprise. Use these tools along with making the cultural and organizational changes necessary to reach the pinnacle.

Competitive Process

Any organization that wants to achieve world-class stature must review its one, two, and three cycles of organizational development. It's estimated that it takes three to seven years for one complete cycle. Therefore, three cycles would take from nine to twenty-one years. A minimum of nine years is needed to ascend from the current reality to the future state and then to the ideal state; this provides the platform for good to great organizations. Moving from stage one—recognizing where you are in the continuum of becoming the best—will take anywhere from three to six months for just the initial assessment. Once you know where you are and where you stand, it will take another six to ten months to agree as a team in figuring out where you want to go after considering your vision, mission, and values as an organization. The next step is to work together as a cross-functional team and decide how to design and to determine the targeted intention of your organization. See Figure 2.3.

Once the goals are set to reach the desired destination, then the same successful methodology could be applied systematically through the entire organization; that is, using the same approaches and deployment tactics pervasive through the entire organizational work units. The competitive process will consist of seven stages after alignment:

1. Alignment of all organizational units
2. Know where we stand
3. Agree where we want to go
4. Design how to get there
5. Roll out the changes

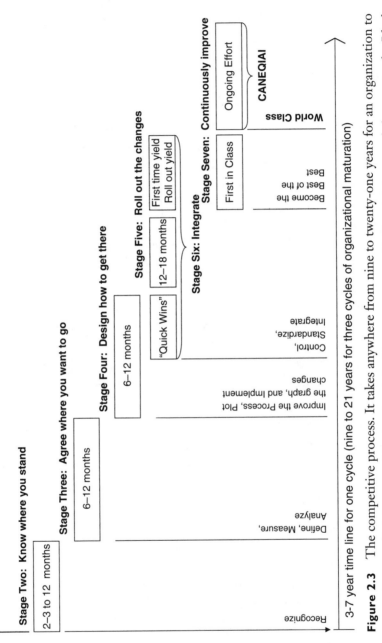

Figure 2.3 The competitive process. It takes anywhere from nine to twenty-one years for an organization to reach the pinnacle of success. Moving from the Present curve, to the Future curve, and then on to the Ideal curve situation is necessary for an organization to become a world-class organization.

6. Integrate a cross-functional process
7. Continuously improve

Competitive Position

Oriel Corporation hosted a Webinar, "Do You Know Your Competitive Position?" in 2007.[6] Speaker Dr. William J. Feuss later extended and expanded the concepts presented in a *Harvard Business Review* article, "Mapping Your Competitive Position.[7] Dr. Feuss presented a methodology called "customer value analysis" and a set of tools that allows any company to chart its competitive position in a way that reveals where you stand relative to the competition on the key performance and price drivers that customers care about. In this Webinar, he revealed many methodologies to help senior executives, marketing executives, and senior managers with responsibility for quality and process excellence to understand how to improve their company's competitive position. Organizations being in a competitive position place their organization to meet the challenges of globalization and world-class competitiveness.

Competitive positions lead to a competitive advantage over competition. This is a good place to be in the fast-changing global market. Organizations must seek any advantage with fact-based, data-driven, data-informed, and knowledge-based information to move from a position of surviving to a thriving one. Here is where the knowledge management expertise and customer resource management described in a later chapter are key to successful endeavors.

WORLD-CLASS PARADIGMS

A world-class organization satisfies a customer by providing a complete packaging of goods, products, and services through an innate understanding of the critical to quality requirements of the customer.

This calls for understanding the precept of a paradigm shift. When there is a shift in a paradigm, everything goes to zero and new concepts are evoked to satisfy new needs and requirements. Organizations must have an understanding of the nature of world-class paradigms to reach world-class stature.

Paradigms are rules or examples we live by that have developed over one's lifetime from various sources that impact our development—such as, upbringing, religion, school, society, and family traits. They help us navigate through the intricacies of life. World-class paradigms include the following:

- Quality—Competitiveness
- Holistic—System thinking
- Attitude—Anywhere, anyplace, anytime
- Agility—Quick to accept change
- Anticipation—Sense of urgency
- Faster—Speed of delivery
- Creativity—Moments of magic (these are customer delighters)
- Understanding—Customer expectations and delivering them (one plus more)
- Continuous quality improvement

An organization must evolve from the current as-is mode of current reality to the next level. This is the should-be condition of the future state. The organization needs to first become a learning and teaching organization, which is a future state of what it should be. Then, it can position itself to elevate its operatives toward the ideal state of what could be, which is being on the continuous quality improvement path, maintaining and sustaining the organization at a high-performance level. This is the world-class operative mode where it is competitive and leading edge. By maintaining and sustaining its improved processes through removal of waste, mistake-proofing, and reducing variance to zero defects, the organization will begin to ascend from a good organization to a great organization.

HOW TO GET TO WORLD CLASS

To reach world-class stature, an organization must build a high-level relationship though the supply chain (supplier, input, processes, output, and customer feedback). The people who are the organization's intellectual capital and greatest asset must have a field of opportunities to use their talents and to harvest the fruits of their labor in an unfettered governance environment. To create a high-performance and an effective organization with operational excellence, each organization must inculcate principle-centered leadership in its top management structure and in its knowledge-based workers in all of its operations and process levels.

Doing the Right Things

If you always do what you have always done, you will always get what you always got. Albert Einstein said, "Insanity is doing the same things over and over again and expecting different results." So why not seek to do things differently and do them right the first time? It reminds me of the quote from Mark Twain, "Why is it that we never have time to do it right, but we have time to do it over." The initial focus for all organization members who aspire to meet this challenge is to create awareness for a world-class operation by doing the right things. Organizations cultivate this by creating empowered, knowledge-based workers and by having these workers look critically at processes instead of tasks.

Business, Operational, and Process Levels

To create a world-class organization there are three areas of additional focus in which an organization must excel. These areas are (1) business, (2) operations, and (3) processes. The following applies to all sectors:

- First, develop knowledge-based workers in a learning and teaching environment who then become world-class employees by building self-equity which in turn builds organizational equity.

- Next, identify the metrics, which are the parameters used to measure progress. Unless an organization is able to measure its performance, it will not be able to gauge its critical success factors, or its key performance indicators.
- Then, begin process improvements by removing waste and variance and by mistake-proofing all processes. This is critical to the success of an organization that expects to be on the leading edge.

Push/Pull Concept

To attain world-class stature one needs to understand customer expectations in terms of the acceptance of a value proposition for the goods, products, and services that are either provided by a supplier or demanded by a customer. The first concept involves a "push" situation where the provider takes the initiative. The second concept involves a "pull" situation where the customer determines the acquisition requirements. An example would be where the supplier pushes a product onto the shelf and the customer pulls the product off the shelf, creating activity for the supplier to restock. Then, if the customer provides feedback about the stock on the shelf, that is another pull having a cognitive impact upon the supplier processes.

Each world-class organization must understand the concept that market forces determine price based upon the profit it expects to get, which is directly proportional to the demand "pull rate" or the customer's perception of a value proposition. Therefore, to attain a world-class competitive edge, an organization must position itself to qualify as a provider of choice. For its own well-being, the provider must be keenly aware of the "pull concept" phenomenon that generates purchasing activity. These activities release a plethora of process requirements that must be considered while streamlining existing processes, which produce the goods, products, and services.

Quality, Cost, and Time

The three-legged stool of quality, cost, and time is significant in a customer's perception of a value proposition. The cost paradigm[8] between the provider and market-driven forces is price determined by the market-driven forces and is more conducive to profit making as the key to the successful operation.

WORLD-CLASS DRIVERS

There are basically three world-class drivers to be developed for an organization to achieve world-class status. These categories are: (1) developing a world-class attitude with respect to work and environment; (2) managing "things" and leading people by focusing on processes to meet the challenges of today's rapid changes in a global economy (our stakeholders are asking us to provide quality products and services better, cheaper, and faster); and (3) providing the appropriate tools and the right kinds of staff training so they become knowledge-based workers for the 21st century.

Three facets are instrumental in an organization's drive to achieve world-class status: (1) the attitude of the people in the organization, (2) the processes through which continuous improvements are achieved, and (3) the tools that the organization chooses to use.

NOTES

1. http://www.quotationspage.com/quote/2474.html.
2. http://www.quotedb.com/quotes/921.
3. Christopher K. Ahoy, "World-Class Operation," *Facilities News Bulletin*, August 1997 (www.fpm.iastate.edu).
4. Sang Lee and Fred Luthans, "Beyond Total Quality Management," Advance Management Seminar, Business Seminars, Department of Management, College of Business Administration, University of Nebraska-Lincoln, 1996.
5. http://www.isc.hbs.edu/firm-competitve.htm.
6. https://www1.gotomeeting.com/register/708843809.
7. William J. Feuss, "Mapping Your Competitive Position," *Harvard Business Review*, November 2007.
8. *The Pricing Paradigm* by Christopher K. Ahoy is in the early development stages.

Where to Start Your Journey

> *"Productivity of the knowledge worker will almost always require that the work itself be restructured and made part of the system."*
> Peter Drucker[1]

It is often difficult to know where to start to create a world-class operation. In order to create an effective organization with operational excellence, we needed to focus on process improvement within the organization. If people are an organization's greatest asset, it does not take much convincing that any organization's intellectual capital, which is its people, must be honed to provide high-level performance. In the end an effective organization needs knowledge workers—good people who give the organization its sustenance vision, mission, and values and who perform with passion and energy. This we must do in order to take the organization to the pinnacle of success: a world-class operation!

EFFECTIVE ORGANIZATION

To create a world-class operation one must begin by creating an effective organization. An effective organization in the 21st century must provide goods, value-added products, and superior services of high quality, at low cost, with delivery that meets the ultimate customer expectations. As a result, the organization receives satisfaction and success for organization design and organizational effectiveness for sustainability in the highly competitive market environment.

OPERATIONAL EXCELLENCE

In the arena of operational excellence, organizations practice total quality management principles, business process reengineering, or business process improvement precepts. In our 21st century, effective organizations are moving from operational excellence to strategic process management. In the arena of strategic process management, organizations use a process-centered or process-oriented organizational design approach. To reach a strategic process management where a process-based competition mode exists, a profound change must take place in an organization before it moves forward. A paradigm shift takes place, and the focus shifts from tasks to processes. When this happens, you know you are on your way to managing processes, which is at the crux of attaining world-class stature through continuous quality improvement.

MANAGEMENT PHILOSOPHY

Modern management science began in the early days with management of doing things, on to the management of direction, and then to the management of results. The scientific management theory propounded by Frederick Winslow Taylor (1856–1915) changed to the management of method, which has ascended to process management in place of organization management. "A completely different thought pattern occurs when you focus your emphasis on the process," states the author H. J. Harrington.[2] Over the years, management philosophy has moved through the following stages:

- Doing (hands on, show-and-tell by supervisors)
- Direction (command and control)

- Result (bottom line)
- Method (today's preferred way to manage is process focused instead of task focused)

In the 21st-century management philosophy, the organization must be centered on process versus task. Instead of looking at the operator creating the error, the focus is on what in the process caused the error. Ask the question, "What caused the error?" and not "Who caused the error?"

Ask, "What does the customer want, need, and require?" Don't just look at the bottom line. Our people must build high-level internal and external successful relationships to create operational excellence resulting in an effective organization.

SELF-EQUITY AND ORGANIZATIONAL EQUITY

There are three precepts in creating a world-class operation. The first is to develop organizational equity by developing individual self-equity. The second is to create the appropriate organization's scorecard for performance measurements. The third is to use the appropriate methodology for process improvement.

The matrix of the success of an organization is in building a staff endowed with self-equity, high-performance operations, and a high level of organizational equity. It is paramount for an employee to understand not merely his or her job responsibilities but also how these responsibilities align with the total processes of the organization. Profound clarity of the organization's values, vision, mission, strategies, and objectives influencing all operations in an effective organization is a must for employees. Assuring process management success of the customer is fundamentally important. Customer satisfaction is no longer good enough. The standard now is *customer success*, a new paradigm for customer success that is built through successful relationships. See Figure 3.1.

Figure 3.1   Successful relationships.

HOW DO WE GET TO THE LEVELS OF NEEDED CHANGE?

This means raising the bar for customer success through the process yields, the Sigma values, and defects per million opportunities, mitigated by solutions provided by removing waste, process optimization, process capability, and design for Six Sigma.

In a customer success environment, the provider is in a continuous and never-ending quality initiative and improvement mode. The provider is learning the customer's business, and teaching the customer to be successful by understanding that the customer's success ultimately translates to self-equity and organizational-equity successes.

In Chapter 7 we discuss what happens when customers do not get the minimum expectation. This is what Noriaki Kano describes in the first zone as the "must be." (Dr. Kano is the developer of a program that provides a ranking system to distinguish essential and differing attributes related to concepts of customer satisfaction, a system which came to be known as the Kano model. The Kano model classifies customer preference into five categories: (1) attractive, (2) one-dimensional, (3) must be, (4) indifferent, and (5) reverse.) The absence of this expectation causes anger on the part of the customer. Very likely customers feel disenchanted with the supplier, and they will not bother to come back to the supplier for future business. The supplier never knows why. The Kano model shows the middle axis as the neutral zone where the organization expects to satisfy the customer with "more than better" service levels. I attribute this to reaching average status or the "should be" position. This is where most companies in the world and in the United States are—usually, just average! On the other hand, in Six Sigma language average companies are at the three-sigma level of capability, which equates to 67,710 defects per million opportunities. The Ahoy model of customer success (see Figure 7.2) indicates three major gaps. These gaps are the result of the differences between current reality and the future and ideal states. The first gap is from the current condition (where the organization needs to go) to the should-be condition. The second gap is created by the difference between the should-be and the could-be conditions. The third gap resides in the area from good to great.

The tools described in Chapter 11 can be used to close these three gaps. Through the system perspective of organizational design, it is possible to attain self-equity for employee development of skill sets using the Baldrige criteria. Self-equity acquired by individuals in the organization then translates into organizational equity. Once an organization's employees have achieved self-equity and organizational equity concurrently, then key performance indicator measures must be put in place to engender success and establish the habit of keeping score, designated as the "dashboards to success" (see Chapter 9). Dashboards provide the appropriate metrics for measurement of critical success factors. To develop appropriate key performance indicators and critical success factors, an organization must have knowledge-based workers, who are well versed in embracing two worlds simultaneously—one world in current reality with mastery of the processes and operatives and the other world in the future state, a world of tomorrow where things should be.

Process yield	Sigma level	Defects per million	Beyond six sigma solution	TRIZ
99.99%	6	3.4	Design for sigma	DFSS
99.98%	5	23.3	Process capability	DFSS
99.4%	4	6210	Process optimization	DMAIC
Lean → 93.3%	3	66807	Waste elimination & Create flow	
Below 93.3%	1–2	308537	Logic & Intuition	EXISTING

DFSS = design for six sigma, DMAIC = devine, measure, analyze, improve and control TRIZ = theory of inventive problem solving.

Figure 3.2 Levels of changes in reaching the Six Sigma level and beyond. (DFSS = design for Six Sigma; DMAIC = define, measure, analyze, improve, and control; TRIZ = theory of inventive problem solving.) Source: Modified from Iowa Manufacturing Extension Program, 2003.

USING SIX SIGMA IN THE TREE OF KNOWLEDGE

There are Six Sigma levels, as shown in Figure 3.2. I created a tree of knowledge indicating the levels of change needed to raise the bar to reach world-class stature. The tree of knowledge is divided into four segments of the various sigma levels for comparison of how an organization must move up the ladder of success by measuring the number of possible defects per million opportunities. The fruit on the ground, the low-hanging fruit, the fruit in the middle, and the fruit at the top depict the levels of attainment as an organization progresses through its quality journey.

To understand how Lean and Six Sigma toolkits are used for problem solutions, the diagram (Figure 3.3) shows a tree divided into four sections. There is fruit on the ground, which indicates a one- or two-sigma level of defects per million opportunities for improvement. Fruit at the lower extremities of the branches depicts a three-sigma level of defects per million opportunities. Fruit at the middle of the tree depict a four- or five-sigma level of possible defects per million opportunities, and at the top of the tree the fruit is equated to just 3.4 defects per million opportunities or a Six Sigma level.

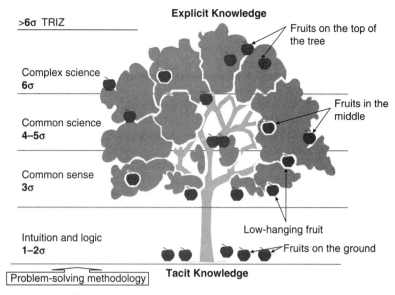

Figure 3.3 Tree of knowledge.

Picking fruit from the ground is equivalent to one or two sigma, which is 668,000 DPMO or 330,000 DPMO, respectively. It may shock you to know that logic and intuition are at one or two sigma, which is equivalent to picking fruit from the ground. Using common sense or picking the low-hanging fruit is operating at a three-sigma level. To get to this level of operation, Lean thinking principles are recommended. Picking the low-hanging fruit in an organization is considered average. Most U.S. companies are average, which means there is room for corrective measures they can take to become world class. World-class organizations are Six Sigma levels of operatives.

Organizations must first seek to arrive at the bottom level of a world-class performance, where meeting customer specifications, or the moment of truth, is like picking the fruit from the middle section of the tree and is considered as attaining the four- or five-sigma levels of performance reaching to Six Sigma level. When an organization reaches this level through common science using organized creative technology, it will have arrived at the threshold of being a good organization—that is, beginning to attain world-class stature. One technology that can be used to check existing conditions to arrive at the should-be level is the DMAIC (define, measure, analyze, improve, and control) process prescribed in the Six Sigma methodologies.

To attain the above world-class levels consistently, an organization must go from being good to being great to being outstanding. It is like picking the sweetest fruit on the tree, which is at the top of the tree, and arriving at the pinnacle. To become a leading-edge organization, the best of the best, an organization must choose to use the DFSS (design for Six Sigma) process improvement.

Two distinct forms of knowledge are needed to improve the organization processes to arrive at the pinnacle of achievement and success. The two kinds of knowledge are tacit and explicit (see Figure 3.4):

1. *Tacit knowledge* is understood or implied without being stated; it is subjective and experience based. It is not expressed in words or formulas; it is know-how, skills, and intuitions, and it is most often embedded in individual members of an organization. It involves know-how, cognitive

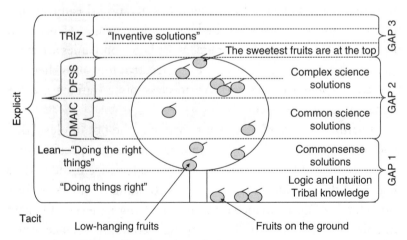

Figure 3.4 Tacit and explicit knowledge.

skills with beliefs, images, intuitions, mental modes, and technical skills in crafts.

2. *Explicit knowledge* is objective and rational knowledge that is expressed in words, sentences, numbers, or formulas. It is information that is easily articulated and communicated. It can be externalized with metaphors, analogies, and mental models, and it can be a combination of databases, documents, and manuals.

Let's look at how to move your organization in the direction to achieve world-class stature.

Each cycle of organizational growth goes through several maturations from pathfinding, aligning, and empowerment. Pathfinding requires an organization to move through the why, what, and how steps to achieve organizational effectiveness.

Why

Arthur Jones (November 1926-August 28, 2007), inventor and founder of Nautilus (exercise machines) and MedX Inc., stated, "All organizations are perfectly aligned to get the results they get." How this statement rings true in achieving the desired results or outcomes! An organization's operative results or outputs are influenced by its core values through a unique set of balanced networks of vision, mission, goals, objectives, strategies, and actions. To achieve long-term improvements with results, an organization must first seek to understand how these key performance indicators interact with each other to produce the current reality. Modify these KPIs to a different configuration to affect change to get the results in the must-do or the should-be future state zone.

What

An organization needs to understand how it is performing today— that is, the current reality. It needs to recognize the problems and issues that facilitate a systemic thinking process where the whole organization is viewed as an ecosystem and where the whole is the sum of its parts and not just a collection of pieces. Stephen Covey says that the interdependency relationships between the key organizational elements and the cause-and-effect value streams influence the desired outcome. The advantage points or the key performance indicators shift the organization's performance through understanding the critical success factors.

How

The diagnoses, treatments, and corrective and preventive actions take place with the customer, stakeholders, and others who may be involved. The process of how to get things done then moves through eight steps: recognize, define, measure, analyze, improve, control, standardize, and integrate. First, an organization must recognize there is a problem; it must define what it is and measure the extent of the problem before analyzing how to improve the process to control the environment or correct the problem to obtain the desired results followed by controlling, standardizing, and integrating the processes to achieve unbiased repeatable results. Since our problems cannot be solved at the same level at which we created them, organizations must develop process improvement methodologies to continuously improve their processes.

PROCESS MANAGEMENT IS A METHODOLOGY

To find the gaps in our processes and to make improvements, we must look at current reality and future goals. Gaps indicate the difference between where we are (current reality) and where we want to be in the future (goals). We may have a long way to go to close these gaps. Finding the as-is conditions and determining the should-be goals will ultimately lead us to the could-be stage. Moving an organization from the must-be condition to becoming "good to great" is a daunting task. To change behavior is an evolutionary, not a revolutionary process. It is the organization's responsibility to determine the gaps in each of these phases. We are looking for and wanting to correct the gaps in our processes.

In either a manufacturing or a transaction process, defects, flaws, or hidden factories are the areas in which to apply the appropriate corrective remedies. There is no way to eliminate waste entirely, even in our personal lives. Look at how much each of us leaves on our plate after each meal. The aggregated accumulated food wasted would be enough to feed many mouths. Despite constant coaching from our mothers from our early childhood to clean our plates because the food that we waste could feed the starving children, we still are plagued with the guilt and the remains of leftover tidbits. The modus operandi "process management" is a methodology for an organization to accomplish its vision and mission in becoming a world-class operation by using appropriate tools. The application of the right tools, metrics, and techniques fulfills this goal by assisting us in managing our processes. See Figure 3.5.

PROCESS MANAGEMENT

A critical issue in many organizations is that frequently managers are not viewing the company as a system or as a whole (Gestalt). Most organizations are focused on return of investments as the systemic end of business. Even though we claim people are our greatest assets, organizations miss balancing this attribute with the humanistic side of things. Most units concentrate on their specific departments or functions, and they are not interested in or even aware of departments and functions that are dependent on them for their existence. Most are focusing their attention on local problems. Focusing just on local problems causes additional problems and frictions with other departments.

If we want to establish good process management for an organization, both short and long term, we must look at process improvement through the lens of a proven mode aligning the seven rights:

1. Right value systems
2. Right core processes

3. Right structure
4. Right people systems
5. Right information systems
6. Right decision-making system
7. Right rewards system

Managing an organization boils down to managing processes.[4] To make constant, continuous quality improvements we must pay attention to process details, making sure we are performing up to our potential. In this hyperspeed, global economy, a holistic, ecological, system-thinking approach is necessary. To compete in a world environment, speed of delivery, cost reduction, and agility to adapt is paramount. To be competitive, we must use metrics and

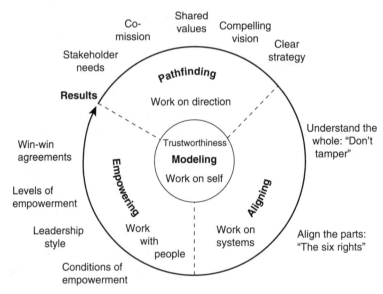

Figure 3.5 The process model.
Source: Dr. Robert Gelina, Center for Continuous Improvement, October 8, 2001, adapted from Steven Covey's lecture "Four Roles of Leadership, Principle-Centered Leadership" and his book, *The Seven Habits of Highly Effective People.*[3]

benchmarks for best practices and discovery and transfer skills to our staff. The key to understanding what we don't know is to use process management in product and services workflow. Six Sigma[5] methodology tells us that:

- We don't know what we don't know.
- We can't do what we don't know.
- We won't know until we measure.
- We don't measure what we don't value.
- We don't value what we don't measure.

NOTES

1. Peter Drucker, *Management Challenges for the 21st Century: Knowledge Work as a System*, HarperCollins, 1999.
2. H. J. Harrington, *Creating Management Philosophy*, McGraw-Hill, 1991.
3. Steven Covey, *The Seven Habits of Highly Effective People*, Simon & Schuster, 1989.
4. See Christopher Ahoy, "Process Management," *Facilities News Bulletin*, Iowa State University, December 1999, available online at www.fpm.iastate.edu.
5. Mikel Harry and Richard Schroder, *Six Sigma: The Breakthrough Management Strategy Revolutionizing the World's Top Corporations*, Doubleday Currency, 2000.

Stages of Change

> *"Change has a considerable psychological impact on the human mind. To the fearful it is threatening because it means that things may get worse. To the hopeful it is encouraging because things may get better. To the confident it is inspiring because the challenge exists to make things better. Obviously then, one's character and frame of mind determine how readily he brings about change and how he reacts to change that is imposed to him."*
>
> King Whitney Jr[1]

CHANGE IS INEVITABLE

We know that change is inevitable in the process of life, and changes are coming faster now than ever before. Change happens and life is full of change, but perfection requires lots of change. The choices are to embrace change and be happy meeting the challenge by taking action, or to resist and be bitter and suffer. Some organization staff members will choose to reassess their personal values relative to their negative positions and will accept the direction their unit is moving to become a world-class operation, or they will choose to leave. Some will choose either to take early retirement or move on to other suitable jobs rather than to go with the flow. A few will still be waiting to see where all this change will lead.

It is the hope of the leadership that those who persevere will actively engage toward our mutual goal to be the best that an organization can be. To reach that goal of being the best, individuals and their organizations need to become competitive and leading edge in their business. All of the knowledge, talents, and experiences are needed in the process of strategic decision making. The formula for this process is $E = MC^2$, where E = enthusiasm, M = motivation, C = commitment, and the second C = contributions to society through the organization's dedicated individuals. All must come voluntarily with a commitment and have an adaptation mindset for individual development of self-equity and organizational equity. This entire endeavor will lead to growth and prosperity for both the individual and the organization, including the ultimate fallout level of customer success for the organization by raising the bar from good to great.

SUSTAINING CHANGE

The difficulty in sustaining change lies in the throes of generating short-term wins, consolidating gains, and producing more needed changes to move the organization through the next levels of excellence (see Figure 3.2). Sometimes, it may take a decade to begin to anchor the organizational changes into the culture. Therefore, the process requires much patience!

THE STAGES OF CHANGE

To reach the stage of the as-is condition an organization must go through stages of change before the individuals and groups arrive at the willingness to commit to the new ways of doing things—to move to doing the "right things." Once the individuals, the teams, and the organization reach the stage of commitment, the rest of the way is basically raising the levels of the bar to reach customer success.

> *"People are not afraid of change, they are afraid of being changed."*
> Unknown Author

From the time an idea or change is introduced, the organization will go through several different stages until the results of the idea or changes are realized. These potentials are optimized if one understands how the life cycle of an organization should perform and how the individual and the entire population of the organization become readied and fitted to reach the pinnacle of the ideal state.

It generally takes three life cycles for an organization to reach maturation in its aspiration to become world class. Then, it needs to sustain this level into the foreseeable future by implementing innovation and differentiation of its goods, products, and services to remain competitive and to maintain its stature through leading-edge process improvements.

GETTING OUT OF THE TROUGH OF CHAOS

To develop a new breed of employee and an organization with a purpose, where people are aligned behind a clearly defined strategy and a compelling vision, requires giving existing workers opportunities to discover their individual talents. It may also require hiring new workers with great attitudes. A friend from Nebraska has a tagline in her e-mail which says, "Attitude not Aptitude Determines Altitude"—very true. We hire staff carefully to assure that they have the right attitude, and then we can work on their aptitude. The organization must capitalize on the strengths and differences of each employee. By pursuing excellence through focusing on individual and organizational strengths while managing the weaknesses, an organization can achieve outstanding results. Many employees will experience much trauma until they accustom themselves to the new ways of working. Some will not be able to make the change.

To get things done swiftly and to create a desire to swim upstream when everyone wants to take the easy road requires preparation with a sense of urgency. One methodology is to establish a guiding coalition for this transformation by using vision and strategies and looking at change assessments.

HOW DO WE PREPARE FOR THIS CHANGE?

Organizations must be in a position of change. The business environment today has changed from that of 20 years ago. In the past, the workforce was not as mobile as today. Some individuals spent their entire career with the same firm, and it was easy to transfer the process knowledge to their successors when they retired— knowledge which they carried in their heads. Today's workforce has changed dramatically along with the processes. Corporations are specializing. Therefore, in the majority of organizations, the idea that each person at a lower level has one specific task and is responsible to make sure that task is performed properly is no longer valid. Accession and succession planning becomes an important ingredient in an organization portfolio.

PROCESS OF GETTING THERE

Going from resistance to acceptance requires an organizational transformation and a personal transformation as shown graphically in Figure 4.1. Organizational transformation involves the following nine-step sequence:

1. Creating employee awareness
2. Establishing a guiding coalition
3. Educating top leaders
4. Building the infrastructure by installing a quality steering committee (advisory board)
5. Focusing on mission, vision, values, and direction for results
6. Educating and training all employees
7. Implementing teams

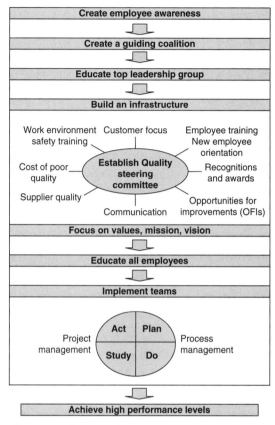

Figure 4.1 Processes for transformation.

8. Planning, doing, checking, acting
9. Achieving high performance

PROCESS FOR TRANSFORMATION

To reach the ideal state of a world-class operation, transformation of an organization must take place at the individual employee level by creating knowledge-based workers and by instituting an organization design. This transformation takes place by:

1. Creating employee awareness by exposing new and existing employees to the precepts of world-class operatives and

developing within the organization an acute awareness of world-class values.

2. Establishing and setting up a guiding coalition to give specific direction to the organization and creating a process for career-pathing and succession planning through a human relations training and development program.

3. Educating top leadership by educating the leadership group in the principles of a world-class organization to help them steer the ship in the right direction by doing the "right things."

4. Building an infrastructure by establishing a steering committee of "pioneers" from all sectors of the workforce who will enable and facilitate the various initiatives.

5. Refocusing on values, vision, mission, objectives, and actions of the organization and accomplishing high performance through building self-equity and organizational equity. Then measuring what matters, and continuously improving processes to achieve world-class stature.

6. Educating and training all employees within the organization to understand world-class competitiveness and leading-edge principles. Implementing collaboration through teams to understand putting into action the processes to remove "silos" and create cross-functional teams.

7. Implement teams and create a safe environment for them to work, removing fear from the organization and creating stable infrastructure with a flatter cross-functional organization. A team approach using a quality steering committee to oversee various quality initiatives will enable operational excellence.

8. Looking at process management through Deming's methodology—plan, do, study (check), and act—and through improving processes, beginning with mapping current reality, the "is" condition.

9. Achieving higher levels of customer satisfaction and success though a results-oriented approach and evidence-driven culture. This is steadfastly observant of a balance between

the systemic analysis and a humanistic approach to a management philosophy.

ORGANIZATIONAL AND PERSONAL TRANSFORMATION

Organizational and personal transition phases can be divided into two categories: strugglers and thrivers. The new century is geared toward the thrivers (organizations or individuals who are in the seat poised to meet the challenges of the 21st century). There are various stages that an individual in an organization may pass through to get to the position of being ready to become a thriver. These are divided into three stages—the victim, the survivor, and the personal. See Figure 4.2.

- *Victim Stage*
  Shock and denial
  Anger and blaming
  Grief and nostalgia

- *Survivor Stage*
  Acceptance of change

- *Personal Stage*
  Reassessment of values
  Commitment and adaptation
  Growth and prosperity

Victim Stage

Shock and denial, anger and blaming, grief and nostalgia are three phases of transition for those organizations or individuals who will be struggling with the changes taking place. During this transition one is left with the feeling that there is no one caring for you, and the impression is that you are alone in this world to tackle the insurmountable odds presented to you on a daily basis. You feel yourself a victim of circumstances. If leadership is focusing with a

Figure 4.2 The process of getting there. (CANEQIAI = continuous and never-ending quality initiative and improvements; pronounced "Can I?")

clear vision to the future, you may feel that others have foisted the impending journey upon you. You did not ask for it or want any change, but it's coming! You are reluctant to let go of the past, and there is inherent resistance to the changes taking place. Grief, anger, denial, and sadness permeate this phase of transition. This is the beginning of going into the ditch of the trough of chaos and confusion.

Shock and Denial

During this transition you are shocked at the circumstances and the predicament you are in. Questions crop up like "Do you think this will really work?" or statements like "It will never fly!" You do not feel this is a real thing happening, and that this too shall pass—perhaps in the blink of an eye. However, slowly but surely you come to realize, and it begins to seep through, that what you are experiencing is not business as usual. The winds of destiny are moving, and you are required to change, because change is inevitable; you can either accept it or be miserable.

Anger and Blaming

This is the stage where you are angry about what is happening, and the tendency is to blame everything around you, along with the circumstances that have brought you this condition. You are not proactive but reactive during this period. The wrath of your anger and blame is dispensed onto everything and anything.

Grief and Nostalgia

Oh, those were the "good old days," sadly no longer here, and you are sentimental about the good things that were just like the familiar tune of a song that voiced, "those were the days my friend. ..." Nostalgia sets in and you are deep into never-never land. Often the bemoaning expressions heard may be, "Just let me do it my way," or "It is much easier the old way." Most of your employees may be in this paradigm for a long time before there is any movement toward the survivor stage.

Survivor Stage

This is the fifth phase of transition and the midpoint of the pendulum of transition where you are generally beginning to accept the changes and starting to live with what is new and seemingly not only doable, but there seems to be new beginnings in the acceptance of change and possible exploration. From the chaos and confusion comes a realization of feeling creative and excited about the future opportunities. This is beginning to make sense. This is the midpoint of Figure 4.2.

Acceptance of Change

Acceptance of change comes when one has passed the point of grieving about the past and is ready to look to the future. At this position, there is hope for the future and the road looks new and exciting and full of promise. One is willing to look at new things and new beginnings with an eye to progress. There are expectations of dreams being fulfilled. This a good stage for any organization, and it is the beginning point of ascending the learning curve.

Personal Stage

This is the stage where exploration seems to be becoming the norm, and it begins to look like you are getting used to and accepting new ways of doing business. It is not really all that bad. In fact, you are beginning to like it. Self-esteem and self-confidence begin to set in and may even lead to preaching this new gospel to others.

Reassessment of Values

At this phase, some employees may wish to be counseled to take advantage of other opportunities that better suit their operating style. A few will begin to question why. Others will find changes too stressful or difficult to continue with the old way. They move on to other opportunities that will better fit their lifestyle. "I don't need this stuff; I will be happier elsewhere."

Commitment and Adaptation

This stage reminds me of a quote often attributed to Goethe, but actually the work of the renowned Scottish mountaineer William Hutchinson Murray:

> **"Until one is committed, there is hesitancy, the chance to draw back, always ineffectiveness. Concerning all acts of initiative (and creation), there is one elementary truth of ignorance, which kills countless ideas and splendid plans: that the moment one definitely commits oneself, then Providence moves too. All sorts of things materialize to help one that would never otherwise have occurred. Whole streams of events issue from the decision, raising in one's favor all manner of unforeseen incidents and meetings and material assistance which no man could have dreamed would have come his way. Whatever you can do or dream you can do, begin it. Boldness has genius, power and magic in it. Begin it now."[2]**

Growth and Prosperity

One life cycle of the human species is from the time you are born to the time you die. However, one life cycle for an organization is generally three to seven years. To reach an ideal state from the current reality, passing though the future state, normally takes three life cycles. It can take from eighteen months to as long as five to seven years for an organization to go from peak to peak. The peaks you are striving to achieve represent the future state for *each* cycle. Your next organizational achievement represents the beginning of a new phase, or life cycle. Future cycles begin as the process of making organizational changes begins to take effect and the organization is taken up another notch.

PROCESS OF GETTING THERE

Figures 4.3 and 4.4 show the pendulum swing from shock and denial, to anger and blaming, to grief and nostalgia, finally reaching the survival stage. Once past this middle marker, the

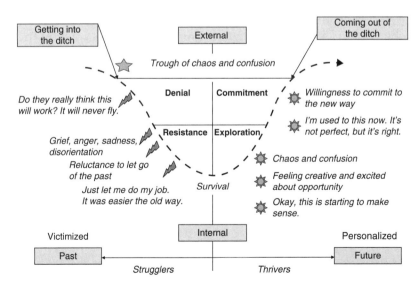

Figure 4.3 Moving through the trough of chaos from the past to the future.

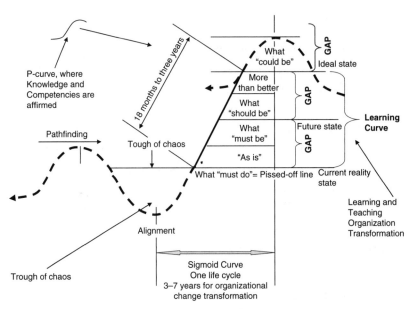

Figure 4.4 The learning curve: organizational change transformation (sigmoid P-curve).

organization will be in the positive curve position (coming out of the ditch) in the trough of chaos, and it now begins behavior modification changes from being victimized to a personalized commitment and to awareness of where the organization is headed. At this stage, the organization is able to move its people past reassessment of "why stay," to where the organization begins to get out of the trough of chaos and into the as-is condition.

NOTES

1. http://www.quotationspage.com/quote/1688.html.
2. From William Hutchinson Murray, *The Scottish Himalayan Expedition*, J. M. Dent, 1951.

CHAPTER

Levels of Development

> *"All growth depends upon activity. There is no development physically or intellectually without effort, and effort means work."*
> Calvin Coolidge (1872–1933)[1]

As we move from the information age to the next level of consciousness, it is evident that we can no longer keep the old philosophy that "one size fits all." Even the ads you see in the stores now state, "one size fits most." The critical success business factors in any organization will depend on management by facts. The metrics of the future to provide customer-driven satisfaction will depend on data derived from information gathered through assessing critical success factors and developing new key performance indicators.

SINGLE CYCLE

For levels of development to happen, we must first look at how an organization goes through a normal cycle. Figure 5.1 shows one biological cycle. Although the biological cycle spans only one cycle, an organization may have opportunities to develop and thrive in multiple cycles during its existence. The diagrams that follow later show three cycles of generations to reach the ideal

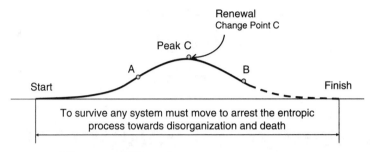

Figure 5.1 The normal life cycle.
Source: Adapted from David P. Hanna (of Procter & Gamble), *Organizations Are the Only Living Systems Who Can Renew Themselves and Thwart Entropy*, Addison-Wesley, 1988.

state condition. How an organization may grow perpetually throughout its existence depends on its ability to rejuvenate itself at each life cycle; otherwise it dies and goes out of business unless positive changes intervene to assist its survival. If a corporation reaches the peak of its one life cycle you must intervene with an initiative for renewal or it will wither on the vine.

> *"To survive, open systems must move to arrest the entropic process. Entropy is a principle describing the movement of all systems towards disorganization and death."*
>
> David P. Hanna,
> *Designing Organizations for High Performance*, 1998

In a later section we will discuss the need for three cycles to achieve the desired results of growth from the current reality, to the future state, to the ideal state. These cycles are shown as P-curves and F-curves in *Mission Possible: Becoming a World-Class Organization* by Ken Blanchard and Terry Waghorn.[2] I added one more, the I-curve, for the tricycle organizational growth that is necessary to sustain growth and to achieve outstanding results, thriving well into the future with unbiased repeatable world-class results.

THE NORMAL LIFE CYCLE

The difference between an organization and a biological living system is that the organization can perpetuate itself literally ad infinitum given the appropriate intervention to grow and prosper. Otherwise, the biological system has a finite life span, caused by the steady degradation of the system. For an organization to be viable and move beyond the survival phases, it must go through three cycles to reach world-class stature. One life cycle for an organization as specified by empirical data is from three to seven years. It moves from the current reality, to the future state, and finally to the ideal state. Then, it must repeat this tricycle state or it will begin to degenerate and disintegrate again. If it keeps renewing itself, it will remain viable, but only as long as its output incorporates sufficient new methodologies to maintain its vantage point will it be a thriving organization.

SIGMOID CURVE

The sigmoid curve (S-curve) shown in Figure 5.2 as the biological life cycle and in Figures 5.3 and 5.4 sums up the story of the time-line of organization life and of our own lives as well. Beginning slowly, we live our lives by experimenting, faltering, and growing—slowly at first, then rapidly; then comes the waxing and waning. It is the product of a life cycle that can be applied to individuals, organizations, dynasties, empires, as well as love and other relationships. In this book we are using three sigmoid curve life cycles for the growth of an organization to reach world class—the P-curve, F-curve, and I-curve.

The sigmoid curve describes the shape of an asymptotically bounded and monotonically increasing function containing exactly one point of inflection.

I use the sigmoid curve to explain using high-performance tools for organizational change and to describe how an organization grows from one cycle, to two, and then to three. The first cycle is

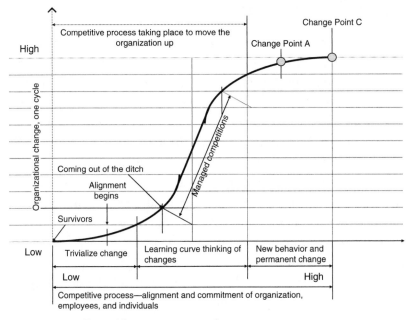

Figure 5.2   Sigmoid curve—one cycle.

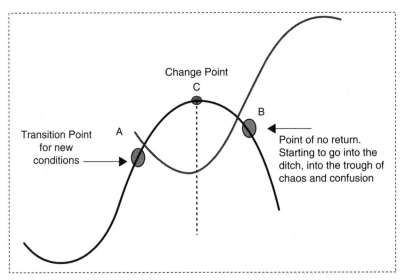

Figure 5.3   The sigmoid curve—change point.

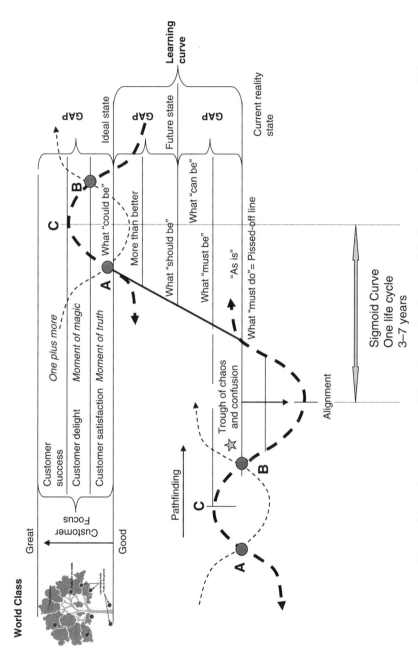

World Class

Great

Customer Focus

Good

Customer success — One plus more
Customer delight — Moment of magic
Customer satisfaction — Moment of truth

GAP — Ideal state

What "could be"

More than better

GAP — Future state

What "should be"

What "can be"

GAP — Current reality state

What "must be"

"As is"

What "must do" = Pissed-off line

Learning curve

Pathfinding

Trough of chaos and confusion

Alignment

Sigmoid Curve
One life cycle
3–7 years

Figure 5.4a   Sigmoid learning curve: one life cycle moving from pathfinding up to the next point of Change A. For a more detailed view of the trough of chaos, see Figure 5.4b on the next page.

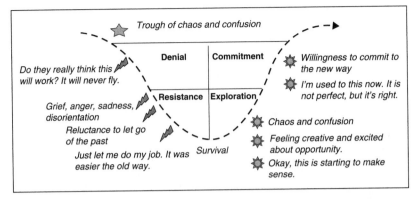

Figure 5.4b Detailed view of the trough of chaos. (You can get stuck in the trough of chaos if you don't keep your focus on your future goals, the peaks, that you are striving to achieve.)

the as-is condition, the second cycle is the should-be condition, and the last cycle is the could-be condition.

P = present, F = future, and I = ideal.

ENTROPIC PROCESS

To survive, any organization must move to arrest the entropic process. An organization is the only living system that can generate itself in perpetuity and thwart the entropic process that a biological system suffers. The P-curve and F-curve described by Ken Blanchard give an impetus toward the sustenance of furthering an organizational life cycle. I add a third life cycle, and call it the *I-curve*. See Figure 5.5. It takes three life cycles for an organization to raise its bar from the current reality state to the future state and, finally, to the ideal state. If the stakeholders wish for the organization to continue to thrive, the organization can then renew itself continuously to maintain itself in perpetuity. But demise of an organization only occurs if it is unable to foresee its future and to determine what it wants to be. Generally, demise starts happening at Point C when the curve starts waning, as shown in Figure 5.3. This need not happen if the P-curve is linked to the F-curve and to the I-curve, as illustrated in Figure 5.6.

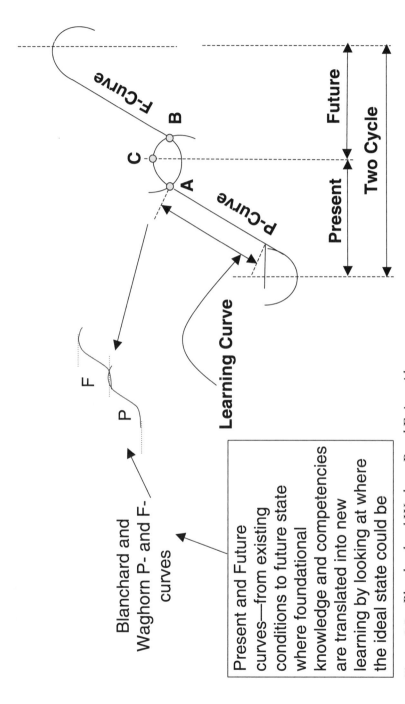

Blanchard and Waghorn P- and F- curves

Present and Future curves—from existing conditions to future state where foundational knowledge and competencies are translated into new learning by looking at where the ideal state could be

Figure 5.5 Blanchard and Waghorn P and F sigmoid curves.

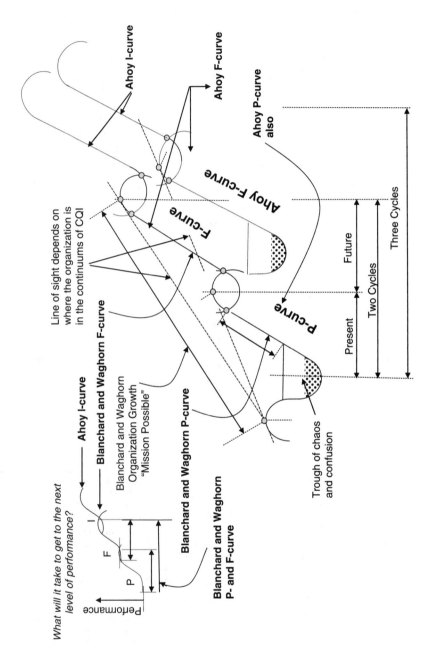

Figure 5.6 Blanchard and Waghorn P and F sigmoid curves plus the Ahoy I-curve.

S-CURVE

Charles Handy says, "Successful industries are constantly reinventing themselves, even when things are going well."[3] He uses the concept of the sigmoid curve to make the case for significant ongoing changes. The sigmoid or the S-shaped curve charts the trajectory of every successful human system. This curve would include an individual or an organization, establishing the required trajectory for success. I am using the sigmoid curve to explain the cycles of organizational development that must take place for any organization to reach world-class stature.

This means moving an organization toward world-class stature using the P-curve (present or current reality state), the F-curve (future state) and adding the I-curve (ideal state), respectively, as three cycles for organizational effectiveness and operational excellence. Becoming an effective organization with operational excellence through process improvements means building high-level relationships and raising the bar at each step from the as-is condition to the must-be condition to the should-be platform (the future state of "more than better") on to the moment of truth or customer satisfaction and ultimately to customer delight, the moment of magic or customer success, which is "one plus more," the ideal state.

P- AND F-CURVES

For an organization to keep on growing successfully, Ken Blanchard talks about the P-curve and the F-curve, the present condition and the future condition, respectively. Handy also says a second curve must start before the first one peaks at point A, when all evidence indicates that there is no need for change to take place. However, most organizations do not change until they get frightened at point B. By then it is too late. System failure occurs, and either the organization dies then or it loses out later to its competition. In these situations most organization leaders have depleted their emotional bank accounts and have lost credibility. With possible depletion of organization resources due to bad planning, leading to further depletion of energy for creative thinking, it becomes difficult to get the organization out of the woods. In the last seven years many Fortune 500 companies have ceased to exist as independent entities, and more are being absorbed because of failure to anticipate the future and determine their ideal state.

CHANGE POINT

At change point A, an organization may go through a period of confusion represented by the shaded area in Figure 5.3 or the trough of chaos represented in Figure 5.4. However, at point C in Figure 5.3, there is an opportunity for an organization to find its path, align, and empower its people to move to the next cycle and not wane as the curve shows toward point B. At this time, there are always two contrasting and competing cultures in an organization. The old culture keepers must produce goods, products, and services with the momentum developed in the first P-curve. The knowledge-based workers who are equipped to straddle both worlds—the current reality P-curve and the future state F-curve—need to keep the profound knowledge in the existing world and look to the future in the F-curve world. In other words, they need to find ways to build that third I-curve while still building upon the successes, learning, and maturity gained from the first or present reality P-curve and the second future F-curve.

The sigmoid curve for one life cycle of the human species is from the time you are born to the time you die. However, one life cycle for an organization is generally three to seven years. To reach an ideal state from the current reality, passing though the future state, normally takes three life cycles. It can take from eighteen months to as long as five to seven years for an organization to go from peak to peak. The peaks you are striving to achieve represent the future state for each cycle. Your next organizational achievement represents the beginning of a new phase (life cycle), Point A in Figure 5.4. Future cycles begin as the process of making organizational changes begins to take effect and the organization is taken up another notch.

P-, F-, AND I-CURVES

An organization must allow the knowledge-based workers to experiment with new ways of doing things, asking new questions to generate new ideas. Charles Handy explains that there is always a first period of experimentation and learning, which is followed by a time of growth and development. Ultimately every curve turns downward (organizations get into the ditch again) and the only thing that varies in each cycle is the length and duration of each part of the curve.

To deter the consequences from the dip cycle, the organization should look at three cycles as a measure of organizational effectiveness while still ferreting out the problems and issues in each cycle of the sigmoid curve—the P-curve, the F-curve, and the I-curve (see Figure 5.7).

When standing at point A in Figure 5.3, an organization is presented with two confusing and opposing views; the questions to ask are "Where am I?" and "Where do I want to go?" Figure 5.4 shows how a typical sigmoid curve behaves within its own cycle. As the organization moves from pathfinding to the trough of chaos and begins to come out of the doldrums in the learning curve section, the organization requires diagnosis and treatment from the perspective of the direction that each individual, leadership, and organization is moving when going from the current reality to the future state.

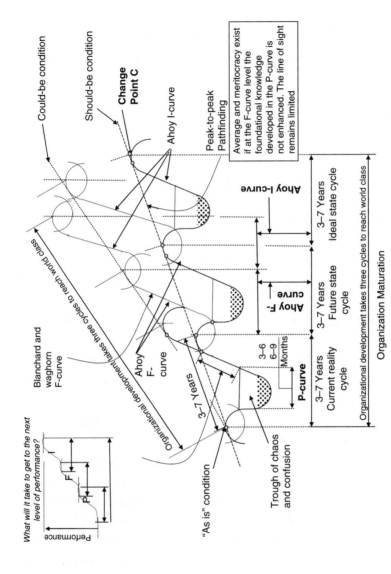

Figure 5.7 Three cycle sigmoid curves (P-, F-, and I-curves)—organization maturation.

USING A SIGMOID CURVE

Using a sigmoid curve to describe one cycle of organizational development is a good graphical example. Figure 5.2 shows a mathematical sigmoid curve, one cycle, and this curve is used to represent an organization's one life cycle depicted graphically in Figure 5.4. The description following Figure 5.4 describes the use of the curve to explain a methodology for alignment and a commitment to sustain competitiveness through short- and long-term strategic thinking. The approach explains a method of personal and organizational alignment and commitment to seek world-class operatives for operational excellence for creating an effective organization by maintaining and sustaining what the organization has gained during the period of its learning curve.

VALUE-DRIVEN PRECEPTS

Value-driven precepts involve permanently changing an organization's culture to reach for outstanding results in the pursuit of excellence, while innovating and differentiating from its competition through continuous and never-ending quality initiatives and improvements. It also involves changing the way employees of an organization think and work together for the greater good. It is about how people are perceived and how they perceive themselves, their organization, their stakeholders, their stockholders, and their customers' perception of the goods, products, and services that they provide.

COMFORT, CHALLENGE, AND CHAOS ZONES

Establishing and sustaining world-class competitiveness requires that the whole organization focus on customer success. This depends upon how the organization develops and deploys its core values and core business processes with a whole system approach, or holistic approach, while harnessing the full potential of its human resources. If one aspires to become world class, it requires an innate, thorough understanding of the three cycles of the life zones to determine what an organization needs to do with its systemic and humanistic resources. See Figure 5.8, which illustrates the three zones.

The three cycles of life zones are exhibited in Figure 5.8. The rings show the three circles of life with respect to work and personal developmental issues:

1. Our comfort zone holds such feelings as certainty and pleasure.
2. Our challenge zone holds such feelings as uncertainty and pain.
3. Our chaos zone, which appears the most troubling and difficult to fathom, provides limitless possibilities and creativity in the area of influence.

The inner ring of the three centric circles is the area where most people reside the moment they are born. Human beings tend to stick to zones where they are comfortable, described later as the certainty area. Most individuals do not naturally like to venture forth into the unknown or to be challenged, described later as

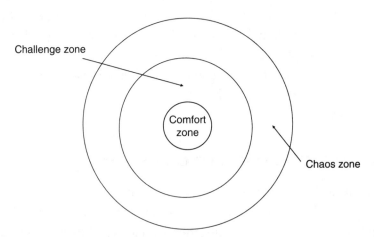

Figure 5.8 Comfort, challenge, and chaos zones: three rings of the life cycle zones.
Source: Geery Howe, M.A., Morning Star Associates (FP&M Leadership Academy, February 2003).

the uncertainty area. However, a few find it exhilarating to possess mastery over their destiny. In the last concentric circle, even though this zone may appear at the outset to be chaotic, the order emanating out of the chaos is the natural law of the universe. This is the area of creativity and productivity where innovation takes place, new questions are asked, new ideas are formulated, and seminal research findings spring forth.

WHAT IS THE COMFORT ZONE?

The comfort zone is a state of pleasure in which an individual or group of people have a natural tendency to reside, thus avoiding pain. One is used to not rocking the boat or looking for new ways of doing things for fear of not getting the results desired. However, in order to attain world-class operatives we need to decrease the size of the comfort zone and increase the space in the challenge zone by taking a courageous step to do things differently; especially, since change is inevitable. Changes create new situations that require new thinking patterns and solutions. When we increase our comfort zone we increase our certainty and pleasure and decrease our uncertainty and pain; however, this leads to complacency. We all want certainty, but maybe the most fascinating place to be in is in the area of uncertainty—the challenge zone. We can cope with uncertainty by being prepared and having mastery of our situation.

Residing in the chaos zone appears to be most confusing, but this is where most creativity takes place. Remember, we are constantly creating order out of chaos. This is the natural state and the order of the universe.

Which path should we choose for success—certainty or uncertainty?

CERTAINTY AND UNCERTAINTY

We immediately enter into a world of certainty and uncertainty during infancy, and continue to manifest our existence in that

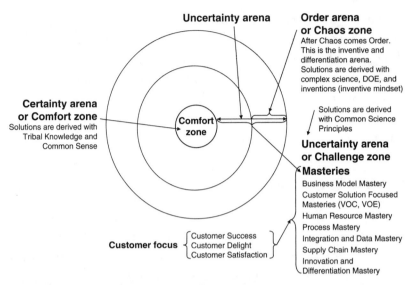

Figure 5.9 Certainty arena (comfort zone), uncertainty arena (masteries zone), and order arena (chaos zone). These are the three rings of an organization's life cycle.

mode. The center of Figure 5.9 shows a comfort zone where most people would like to reside—the area of certainty and pleasure. Homilies like "Don't rock the boat," "Don't fix it if it ain't broke," "I am comfortable here; why do I need to change?" are in the inner circle where we seek refuge. But to move from the "is" condition of the current reality state to the future state of what "should be," we must move from the certainty circle to the uncertainty. This is the uncertainty arena, or challenge zone.

CHALLENGE ZONE OR MASTERY

Craft mastery is to develop profound knowledge—knowledge both explicit and tacit—as well as to acquire the requisite skill sets to solve the commonsense and common science problems that put us in a position to handle more complex science problems. The challenge is to build strength and core competencies to get out of the rut or current reality. We can then take action and solve the problems of tomorrow. To reach the ideal state is to design and implement solutions where there is no blueprint to follow. One example of craft mastery can be watched on the current TV series the *Monster Garage* or the motorcycle mechanics' *American Zone*. These supermechanics are confronted with a problem and given the requisite budget and materials to complete a task. The task is to build a machine that operates and competes with existing machinery. Time and time again the supermechanics were able to produce and outwit their competitors and build something never before accomplished because each has a mastery of the craft to be able to design and implement an integrated plan to build machinery that operates above the current standards. The new global economy requires perfecting seven critical "masteries" as follows:

1. Business model mastery
2. Customer solutions focus mastery
3. Human resources mastery
4. Process mastery
5. Integration and data mastery
6. Supply chain mastery
7. Innovation and differentiation mastery

BUSINESS MODEL MASTERY

Business model mastery requires an honest, open, and transparent values-driven organization with proactive methodologies and value propositions from various sources of suppliers, inputs, outputs, outcomes, and customers that form strategic alliances and partnerships. With these masteries the organization is positioned to deliver goods, products, and services with the possibility of providing its customers the world-class capacity and capability to balance revenue and growth opportunity solutions with high-quality, low-cost, and speed-of-delivery production. Hence, business model mastery is seeking value propositions for customers proactively through data mining and the delivery of a holistic systems approach to solutions. We must position our organization to respond to segmented, market-driven conditions to determine the capabilities and capacities needed by any organization to deliver goods, products, and services—better, cheaper, faster.

When we at Iowa State University's Facilities Planning and Management department (FP&M) shared what we were doing and what we had achieved together as a team, many groups made a special journey to visit us and see for themselves what we do and how we do it. That the best practices we introduced into our organization are needed and desired by many was evidenced by the feedback that we received from our travels and from the comments we received from our visitors.

CUSTOMER SOLUTIONS FOCUS MASTERY

Customer focus has three areas of customer-centered wants, needs, and requirements. Beginning at the lowest level of goods, products, and services is satisfaction, followed by delight and success.

Customer focus mastery concentrates on understanding what customer satisfaction, delight, and success parameters are and on fulfilling the voice of the customer through value-added products and services. This mastery is based on mass-customized products and services, possible self-directed or self-managed logistics with a provision of full, life-cycle product management from cradle-to-grave, womb-to-tomb, or cradle-to-cradle—in some instances guaranteeing superior total cost of ownership instead of first cost.

HUMAN RESOURCES MASTERY

Creative human resource activities focus on developing workforce systems, workforce engagements with diversity, emphasis on ethnicity, and in developing capacity and capabilities. Find talents and provide fields of opportunities with a constant introduction of new tools, equipping employees to be able to develop skills, experience, and knowledge, thus enabling staff to grow and to be successful, building on strengths and coping with weaknesses.

Human resource mastery is continuous development and training to provide new tools and skills to enable employees to become future leaders and to be successful at what they do. Workforce systems, management, and engagement play a major role in continuous process improvements. The right people, patience, perseverance, and persistence in methodologies play a major role in developing the appropriate workforce engagements.

PATIENCE, PERSEVERANCE, AND PERSISTENCE

Ideas take time to gel in any endeavor and especially an organization that has perpetuated doing things right for a long time. Patience, perseverance, and persistence are the key ingredients to reaching your goals.

PROCESS MASTERY

If we are to survive successfully in our ever-changing world, we necessarily need to be avant-garde to meet tomorrow's challenges. We must look at processes internally as well as externally. We must secure best practices through metrics and benchmarking for comparative analysis, and communicate the acquisition of new skills, experience, and information to others throughout the organization. To obtain competitive advantage in the evolution of process management, companies are moving from total quality management and business process reengineering, which is operational excellence, to being a learning organization[4] and being able to manage processes up and down the value chain, as seamlessly as possible.

INTEGRATION AND DATA MASTERY

Integration and data mastery introduces SMART (specific, measurable, accountable, responsible, and timely) information, which is accurate, on time, up-to-date, real-time (one version of truth), fact-based, data-driven, data-informed, and knowledge-based and includes event-driven metrics, enabling organizations to make the right decisions at the right time and place as quickly as possible.

Data collection and data mining is an inherent part of the process to assure that the organization is measuring what matters. Unless ones measures, it will not mean anything. As Lord Kelvin (William Thomson, First Baron [1824–1907]) said:

> "When you can measure what you are speaking about and express in numbers, you know something about it. But when you cannot measure it, when you cannot express it in numbers, your knowledge is of a meager and unsatisfactory kind. It may be the beginning of knowledge, but you have scarcely, in your thoughts, advanced to the stage of science."

SUPPLY CHAIN MASTERY

Supply chain mastery combines flexibility, responsiveness, and social and spiritual value-stream mapping of the work flow processes. It provides just-in-time inventory, rapid cycle adjustment, and quick response with instantaneous readjustment up and down the total value-stream processes. Hence, supply chain mastery is assuring that the value-streaming synchronization of both products and services with social value streaming instigates quick response with flexibility and responsiveness to both the voice of the customer and the voice of the employee.

INNOVATION AND DIFFERENTIATION MASTERY

Innovation and differentiation mastery uses the theory of inventive techniques modeling for radical improvement—raising the bar for high performance and building best practices which are extremely difficult for the competition to replicate in a timely manner.

Innovation and differentiation mastery refers to making radical changes or establishing new parameters for products, programs, services, processes, or organizational effectiveness, creating a new value for stakeholders different from that currently in vogue. It may be an adoption of an idea, process, technology, or product line that is either new or new to its proposed application and different from that which exists. At times the word *uniqueness* may enter the realm of innovation and differentiation since the new solution may be one of a kind and one that the competition has not been able to emulate.

Organizations that innovate and differentiate their goods, products, or services from the competition may use many steps that involve development and knowledge sharing. Although often innovation and differentiation are used in product manufacturing sectors with technological innovation or differentiation, the methodology that benefits the organization is applicable to all processes.

Mastery of innovation and differentiation may involve major structural and paradigm shifts in approach or output that require fundamental changes in organizational structure or business models. Those who change the way business is conducted to outwit competition become the best of the best and assure continued effectiveness of the organization with high-performance operational excellence.

SUPERIOR GOODS, PRODUCTS, AND SERVICES MASTERY

The customer is looking for superior goods, products, and services mastery—using the "better, cheaper, and faster" mantra for all transactions with the cash-conversion-cycle mindset and delivering total solutions to the customer-success parameters for the customer's entire enterprise.

WHAT IS THE CHALLENGE ZONE?

The challenge is to learn to cope with uncertainty through developing capacity, capability, and expertise as well as mastery for dealing with a variety of circumstances. The challenge is to understand business through profound knowledge and to "test the waters" constantly for continuous quality improvements. Challenges for the individual and the organization are to find the right mix for the parameters of commitment, participation, satisfaction, complexities, resources, qualities, values, vision, mission, objectives, strategies, implementations, time, cost, and risk.

WHAT IS A CHAOS ZONE?

When we venture into the area of chaos, we might be in the best area of all three zones because this is the greatest area of uncertainty. Creativity abounds in this zone of the unknown, which is the most exciting for opportunities and possibilities. Sending a rover machine to Mars is an example of possibly working things out in this lunatic fringe, and it is the most exciting adventure—creating order out of chaos.

WHAT ARE THE CONSEQUENCES OF THE STATUS QUO?

Guaranteed: if we stay in our comfort zone, we will loose our edge! We must assess current reality, the as-is condition, which is also the current condition. In our organization, we succeeded by mapping processes, making the bold move by making changes through *kaizen* events (good change), and then we made progress by using commonsense practices of removing waste, and then moving on to the common science methodology of problem solving and optimizing our process improvement issues. This is the future state or should-be condition, and then we needed to reach for the stars—the ideal state or the could-be condition—by using complex science.

COMFORT ZONE, MASTERY ZONE, AND CHAOS ZONE

In the world of physics there is a universe of related things, and one typical pattern that appears to run in the universal system is the binary functions and the rhythm of three rows of events. For instance, binary functions may be fast or slow, high or low, right or wrong, happy or sad, on or off, etc. The rules of three are like three legs of a stool—the triangle figure, three angles in a triangle; quality, cost, and time; better, cheaper, and faster; fact-based, data-driven, and knowledge-based; attitude, process, and tools; competency, collaboration, and communication; scope, budget, and expectations; common sense, common science, complex science, and so on.

In the same vein, certainty and uncertainty are two binary factors intertwined with each other from the moment we take our first breath of air at birth. The doctor or the midwife slaps our bottom to assure that first cry. From then on the remarkable human body, guided by our brains, begins to teach us the techniques for our survival in this world, ruled by logic and intuition. Logic and intuition are on the one- and two-sigma scale. This is like picking the fruits from the ground in the diagram of the tree of knowledge.

Figure 5.9 shows several steps in the states of personal and organizational transformation, moving from the comfort zone to the mastery zone, the area of expertise and capabilities. Once an organization reaches this state, the individuals in the organization have tacit knowledge. The individuals and organizations are then positioned and ready to move into the last developmental phase— the chaos zone from which stems the order of things. The area of chaos and confusion stimulates creativity for producing goods, products, and services that are innovative and differentiated from the competition.

WHAT TO DO?

Using the Lean Sigma way, value-stream mapping is created. New maps are produced through kaizen events that move process improvement through the continuous improvement cycles from the as-is condition to the should-be condition to the could-be condition—arriving at the threshold of a good organization positioning itself to become a great organization. Organizations that begin the journey from good to great are potential world-class organizations.

Strengths, Weaknesses, Opportunities, and Threats

Information to make an informed judgment is derived through a grounded understanding of the critical success factors that provide key measurements known as key performance indicators. Business at the speed of thought is the norm. This norm demands that quality products and services be delivered cheaper and faster with improved quality. Unless an organization is agile and changes to meet today's challenges and opportunities, it will not become a world-class operation. Leaving things as is because they have worked in the past is not a viable organizational modus operandi. To be a viable organization, we need to take action to spur change for continuous improvement. Therefore, "If it ain't broke, change it" becomes the new paradigm for the 21st century. (See Chapter 8 for an extended discussion.)

To be competitive in business, we need all the knowledge, talent, and experience we can muster for the strategic decision-making process. Strategic decisions are possible only after understanding the matching processes that are derived after doing an environmental scan of the economic and political impacts on the growth of an organization. We need to understand that changing or modifying behavior to meet the challenges of the 21st century is a must. Enthusiasm and motivation must come voluntarily. A road map is necessary to guide an organization in its quality journey toward achieving world-class stature and customer success. The road map can only be developed after an organization drills down deeply by looking at its strengths, weaknesses, opportunities, and threats. The integration of the processes through external trends analysis; internal capacity analysis; and reviewing of core values, vision, missions, objectives, and strategies generates the strategic and tactical decision making and action plans

STRATEGIC DECISIONS

Strategic decisions are made at the leadership level. Strategic decisions are derived from matching three different decision-making processes. These components are environmental opportunities that are placed before an individual or an organization. The environmental opportunities and constraints are very much externally driven forces that may be beyond the realm of control of the individual or the organization. These decisions are at times a result of the political climate or of the environment in which the program is impacted. The SWOTs are in an area in which an organization makes the most productive and meaningful changes possible. The third item of personal values, shown as a component, is the difficult one to resolve. It is the most difficult of the three ingredients that go into the mix in Figure 5.10, and it shakes up the processes to create the effective and efficient strategic decisions that lead to desired future outcomes. "Leadership finds meaning in every step of the way, from finding and seizing opportunities to making strategic decisions."[5]

Figure 5.10 aptly shows what an organization has to face to elevate its position in the universe of making strategic decisions.

During the writing process, I was excited to discover a decision-making software tool called "Decision Lens" (see description below) that could allow any organization to scientifically make its strategic decisions. However, if necessary, the decisions made using this software could later be adjusted (for political or policy

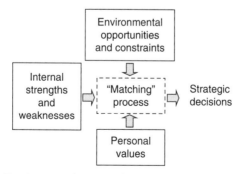

Figure 5.10   Decision-making model.
Source: "Creating a World-Class Operation," lecture by Christopher Ahoy. © 1997 *Ahoy Lecture Series*.

reasons) and supplemented by human intervention the traditional way. In other words, you will be able to first choose through a scientific prioritization using this software and then use political acumen to make the adjustments if needed after the software has eked out the solution.

DECISION LENS OVERVIEW

Decision making is the most critical driver in determining whether an organization succeeds or fails. Decision Lens is a software platform based on the leading theory in decision making for prioritization called the *analytic hierarchy process* (AHP). The AHP is unique in its ability to bring together the knowledge and experience of a group, to collaboratively develop a set of objectives as a hierarchy, and to apply the individuals' knowledge, experience, or data through a set of relative comparisons (called *pairwise comparisons* with each element compared in importance to the others). Through this rational set of trade-offs, Decision Lens enables decision makers to evaluate both quantitative and qualitative objectives by asking which is more important and by how much (1–9 scale). The result is a set of priorities with weights showing their relative importance to one another. These priorities are then used to evaluate investments in products, programs, or projects.

Decision Lens works with leading organizations such as Johnson & Johnson, eBay, Amtrak, Joint Chiefs of Staff, Navy, Air Force, and others to bring structure and quality to their key decisions. Decision Lens offers a family of open, integrated solutions that enable organizations to easily and effectively:

1. Organize and evaluate complex factors contributing to a decision and to prioritize the alternatives for the best outcome.
2. Reduce the amount of time and money to make effective decisions.
3. Accelerate consensus building and ownership while applying the collective intelligence of key stakeholders in a decision.

4. Synthesize quantitative and qualitative benefits, opportunities, costs, and risks of alternatives into decisions.
5. Spend your resources well. Allocate your limited resources to get the most value for your organization.
6. Remove stress and uncertainty often associated with complex and significant decisions.
7. Quickly test the impact and sensitivity of changing scenarios on business decisions.
8. Provide transparency into how decisions were made.
9. Establish sustainable and higher-quality decision-making processes.

NOTES

1. http://www.quotationspage.com/search.php3?homesearch=development.
2. Kenneth H. Blanchard and Terry Waghorn, *Mission Possible: Becoming a World-Class Organization*, McGraw-Hill, 1997.
3. Charles Handy, *Understanding Organization*, Penguin Business Library, 2005.
4. Peter M. Senge, *The Fifth Discipline: The Art and Practice of the Learning Organization*, Doubleday/Currency, 1990.
5. Christopher K, Ahoy, *Leadership in Educational Facilities Administration*, Alexandria, VA, APPA 2007.

CHAPTER

Who Is the Customer?

> *"Creating raving fans: Satisfied customers just aren't good enough."*
> Ken Blanchard (1993)

A customer is a person or group that buys goods, products, or services and with whom an organization has a relationship. According to Wikipedia, the word *customer* historically meant "habit." The customer was someone who frequented a particular shop, who made it a habit to purchase goods there, and with whom the shopkeeper had to maintain a relationship to keep the "custom"—meaning the continuation of expected purchases in the future. Customer satisfaction implies a condition that is free of doubt, suspicion, or uncertainty in the mind of the customer. This established condition assumes that the customer's wants, needs, and requirements are met based upon standards of expectations of form, fit, and function. The customer, not the provider organization, determines these standards.

> *"The customer may not always be right, but the customer is always the customer."*
> Christopher Ahoy,
> Lectures—"Creating Awareness for
> World-Class Operations," 1997

117

Save yourself considerable time. Learn not to get caught up in whether the customer is right or wrong. What matters is the commitment that your organization has to provide wants, needs, and requirements of the customer. Meeting and exceeding customer expectations through delivery of world-class goods, products, or services through a superior relationship is the name of the game. Superior service and a high-level relationship depend on knowing that customers are:

- The most important visitors on our premises.
- Not dependent on us. We are dependent on them.
- Not interruptions of our work but the purpose of it.
- Not outsiders to our business but a part of it.
- Not doing us a favor but giving us an opportunity to serve.

VOICE OF THE CUSTOMER

Listen to the voice of the customer; check "fitness to need" with better understanding of customer wants, needs, and requirements; and provide the goods, products, or services that raise customer success.

The three sources for money origination in a viable organization are shareholders, financial institutions (banks), and customers. Many organizations have shareholders who are dissatisfied about constantly putting more money into investments without positive results. Banks or financial lending institutions will only commit their financial resources as long as they see a good return on investment. Customers only will pay what they feel is appropriate and fair for goods, products, and services that are of high quality, low cost, and delivered when they want them.

A viable organization satisfies all these sources. All organizations are entitled to produce goods, products, and services of high quality, lower cost, and faster delivery and make a reasonable profit. All three entities must come together for a common purpose in support of each other's needs so as to receive optimal benefits.

Such conditions depict entropy where the right kind of environment must exist for all independent variables to operate at the maximum potential. Raising the bar for customer success challenges the enthalpy conditions (see Chapter 7).

In creating customer success through a world-class operation, the crux of the issue is that we need to ask good questions: (1) What kind of organization will be in a position to achieve world-class stature? (2) Why do we need to create productivity excellence and high-performance? (3) What needs to be done to create an effective organization? (4) What must we determine when we go about attaining this world-class operation?

LISTENING TO THE VOICE OF THE CUSTOMER

If an organization hopes to achieve customer success, it must start by listening critically to the voice of the customer. To acquire world-class stature, an organization must understand the critical-to-customer needs, requirements, and satisfactions. Understanding the VOC is critical to the success of any enterprise. Knowing that the ultimate goal for any enterprise is relationship building, motivated organizations will launch a quality journey by improving everyday processes. There are three conditions that organizations must seek to achieve customer satisfaction or delight. These are (1) having the right people in the organization with the right attitude, (2) having the proper processes in place, and (3) using the right tools to attain a competitive advantage.

LISTENING TO THE VOICE OF THE EMPLOYEE

If an organization hopes to achieve customer success, it must start by listening critically to the voice of the employee. To acquire world-class stature, organizations must have happy and educated employees, critical-to-customer needs, requirements, and satisfaction. Understanding the voice of the customer is critical to the success of any enterprise.

LISTENING TO THE MANY VOICES OF THE CUSTOMER

The many different and differing voices of the customer are important to the organization. It is critical in this competitive environment to listen carefully. Asking the right questions to get the best answers is really important in scenario planning. To be responsive to the customer's critical wants, needs, and requirements, it is equally important to determine exactly why to do something, what to do, and how to do it. An organization must put in place a systematic methodology to capture these voices and to understand what the customer is saying.

In this global economy more and more competitive enterprises are focusing on the voice of the customer. It does not matter how good you are and how perfectly you can produce goods, products, and services. If the production does not meet your customer's expectations, your customer is unhappy. Then, you or your organization will have failed to meet the customer's wants, needs, or requirements. If the voice of the customer is not heeded, an organization will miss the opportunity of understanding the customer's critical-to-quality requirements. This will lead to an inordinate amount of wasted time and resources by needlessly supplying frills that may not matter at all to the customer—frills that you must also maintain and monitor in the future.

For example, if you are a supplier of computer software and you volunteer frills that were not requested in the customer's requirements document, the documentation may not be in the user's best interests. However, you are obligated to maintain those frills (at a cost to you) for the life of the product. Listening to the voice of the customer is a critical aspect of doing business well. For example, in the facilities arena no matter how efficient a job is done by the facilities personnel in remodeling by using the latest and best fixtures, materials, and systems to make the room as perfect as can be, if the customer is not happy with the outcome, then one has missed an opportunity to really listen to the voice of the customer and the problem is not resolved. It may be that your customer's perceptions or expectations are different from yours and you will need to find out what it is to get to the root cause. All the excellence in processes improvements and superior services provided will mean very little. If such a situation is anticipated to arise, you need to know how to handle these circumstances; otherwise you will have missed an opportunity to get it right the first time. There may not be a second chance. Not listening to the voice of the customer to determine the wants, needs, and requirements of the customer is something an organization must take heed of if it wants to keep that customer. Understanding customer requirements is key to a successful relationship.

CUSTOMER REQUIREMENTS

Most organizations generally understand customer requirements, which are sometimes known as *critical-to-customer requirements* (CCRs). These requirements are minimal conditions that organizations must meet. Some CCRs do not always cater to a customer's expectations where the customer is actually focusing on his or her needs or wants. Conditions may shift due to variations at the supply chain and at the input level before a process takes shape in five areas—people, machine, material, method, and environment. The globalization of our world and the new e-economy are fostering and pushing for changes at breakneck speed. The diversity of our population and the diminishing cultural boundaries are manifesting newer wants, needs, and requirements, not easily perceptible to the uninitiated. The climate is ripe for clarifying the unique customer wants, needs, or requirements in each situation and discovering how best to accommodate customer success for any organization aspiring to become the best.

Customer requirements surpass customer wants and needs. In other words, customer requirements trounce all other situations, as they are critical to supplying the minimum requirements that will fulfill the customer's expectations. An organization must translate these critical requirements through a tool known as *quality functional deployment* (QFD), which made its first appearance in the automotive industry. QFD is also known as the "house of quality." It is a structured methodology of translating customer requirements into technical specifications for each step of the development of a product or service. These include design, manufacturing, and implementation of various processes to capture the voice of the customer.

The QFD matrix includes identification, verification, and clarification of the following:

1. The voice of the customer (wants, needs, and requirements).
2. The importance of customer requirements as differentiated from wants and needs.
3. Product characteristics to meet customer requirements.
4. Correlations between the required technical specifications of the products or services with customer requirements (relative importance rating with respect to correlation as evaluated through a weighing system).
5. The weighing correlation between customer requirements and product and services characteristics.
6. Prioritization of customers' perception of products and services produced by the organization as compared to the organization's competition.
7. The level of customer focus throughout the organization.

CUSTOMER SERVICE—MEETING THE SPECIFICATIONS

The most traditional methodology for training salespeople is to have them learn to meet customer specifications. Meeting customer specifications is commonly known as "customer service." This would have been enough in the old days if there was no competition. Customers would have to take whatever the supplier produced at whatever levels of quality, cost, and delivery. However, with the increasing number of suppliers, globalization, and more industry competition, suppliers have to provide goods, products, and services better, cheaper and faster.

The customer has many choices if not satisfied with the type of products or services being provided. They can go to wherever they can find vendors who will be able to meet or exceed their expectations. An organization arriving at the threshold of being good (that is, customer satisfaction) will find that being good is not enough. Customer satisfaction—arriving at the moment of truth for most organizations is just a stopping point. It is the beginning of the journey from good to great.

CUSTOMER SATISFACTION—MOMENT OF TRUTH

For many companies, customer satisfaction is the single most important issue affecting organizational survival. Despite this fact, most companies have no clue of what their customers really think. Organizations that are not prepared to meet the challenges of tomorrow operate in a state of ignorant bliss, believing that if their customers were anything less than a hundred percent satisfied, they would hear about it. This is not so. Since most customers migrate to areas where they are more comfortable, they do not need to confront the issue. The supplier companies are shocked when their customer base erodes. Their existence is threatened, and they have no idea why. If customers are unhappy with the service, even loyal customers, they tend to purchase elsewhere. They do not need to go through the hassle of not having their wants, needs, and requirements met. They simply purchase from other vendors. How often we hear an expression like "I just don't understand; we did everything we could to satisfy our customers and to meet their specifications."

Meeting specifications is reaching the zone where an organization begins to understand what it takes to reach customer satisfaction. This is known as arriving at the *moment of truth*. This is also the 1SO 9000 level of scrutiny for an organization. Just meeting ISO 9000 verification and clarification of meeting standards is not enough. Arriving at the moment of truth, knowing what it takes to satisfy customers, may not be enough to keep their loyalty or to meet their minimum expectations.

CUSTOMER SATISFACTION MODEL (KANO MODEL)

The three categories of quality items that affect customer satisfaction are "dissatisfiers," "satisfiers," and "delighters." These categories were originally developed in 1984 by the Japanese quality guru Professor Noriaki Kano. He initially introduced a two-factor, quality model commonly known as the *Kano Curve*.

The Kano Model of Customer Satisfaction as shown in Figure 6.1 divides product attributes into three categories: threshold, performance, and excitement. A competitive product meets basic attributes, maximizes performance attributes, and includes as many "excitement" attributes as possible at a cost the market can bear and one that the customer values.

CUSTOMER SUCCESS MODEL (AHOY MODEL)

The Ahoy model portrayed in Figure 6.2 is a Kano/Ahoy model merge, which determines that the bottom line or Kano's "must be" is Ahoy's "must do" quadrant. The bottom line is the current reality and the current state of affairs. This "is" condition will vary with generational differences, country of origin, diversity, and cultural mores. In other words, customers will be very angry if they do not get what they expect from the goods, products, or services that they value to meet their wants, needs, or expectations.

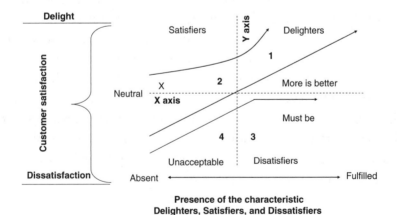

Figure 6.1   Noriaki Kano's customer view of quality—dissatisfiers, satisfiers, and delighters (modified by author to include the four quadrants for discussion purposes only).

The purpose of the Ahoy model is to advance understanding of how an organization's modus operandi will achieve the higher levels of performance through customer focus. Figure 6.2 shows how organizations that achieve world-class status must move from the minimum conditions of the current reality, to the as-is condition, to the next level of ascendancy to reach the should-be condition, the future state, then moving onward to the could-be condition, the ideal state, arriving at the level of the moment of truth. This is the "good" situation where expertise acquired takes an organization to the bottom of world class, reaching the "ideal" state that everyone can expect to reach at maturity. Arriving at this level of the moment of truth is the satisfaction zone, where organizations are meeting ISO 9000 specifications or meeting standard operating procedures.

The customer satisfaction journey with the Kano model comprises moving an organization from the dissatisfaction area, past the neutral or average zone, to customer delight. The Ahoy model expands this concept in Chapter 7, where customer satisfaction or Kano's customer delight situation is the transition point for an

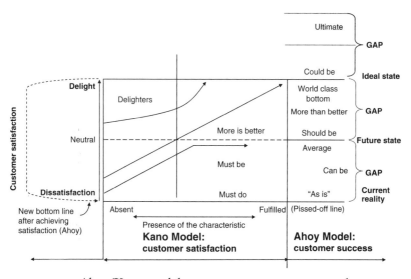

Figure 6.2 Ahoy/Kano model merge—customer success and customer satisfaction model.

organization moving from customer satisfaction to delight, then to success, poised to perform outstanding results.

CUSTOMER DELIGHT—MOMENT OF MAGIC

Organizations, large and small, are seeking to narrow or eliminate many "gaps" in their current reality state and in their future state, as well as in their ideal state. With the assistance of knowledge-based workers, it is possible to reach the future state and the ideal state from a current reality paradigm. It is necessary to achieve a world-class status, moving from an as-is condition to the must-do, must-be, can-be, should-be conditions, and to more than better, to could-be conditions—meeting customer expectations or meeting and exceeding those expectations—to be able to reach the "customer delight" paradigm and eventually arriving at the ideal state or desired outcome, where the playing field is for high-performance organizations. The stage at which the moment of magic is attained is for excellent organizations, which is best described by a story:

> A lady drove up to a **Nordstrom** store in Fairbanks, Alaska, walked up to the counter, and demanded that the tires she had purchased a few months back for her truck be replaced since they were too soon worn and threadbare. The salesgirl was taken aback with the request but quickly composed herself. She had been coached to take care of such unusual circumstances and brought this matter to the manager. Gathering her wits together, she asked the lady for her keys, gave her some coupons for shopping, and asked her to return in an hour. The manger sent another employee to Sears to have the truck fitted with new tires. Within the hour the tires were replaced without question and the customer was handed her keys and the receipt. When she returned home, the customer looked at the invoices for her purchases and to her surprise discovered that Nordstrom's, where she had complained about her tires, had not only given her $80 worth of coupons but had replaced her tires without any cost

to her even though they do not sell tires. Nordstrom's replaced her tires at Sears at a cost of $180 while she was happily shopping, spending the coupons and her own money. Just imagine the chagrin when she discovered that she had gone to the wrong shop to have her tires replaced followed by great embarrassment and appreciation! This was a moment of magic; it pays to go an extra mile and please your customer, who may be loyal for life for this special service. Although there are many versions of the tire story, this bit of folklore is the one I heard when I was living in Fairbanks, Alaska. The message is that the customer is always right. A world-class organization does whatever is appropriate and needed to heed the voice of the customer.

Many companies while attempting to fulfill their obligations to customers' wants, needs, and requirements are now delving into the art and science of customer relations management, which has come into vogue as a necessary function of thriving organizations.

CUSTOMER RELATIONS MANAGEMENT

One of the central premises of customer relations management (CRM) is that customers are all different. An organization must be primed to meet different wants, needs, and requirements of the customer through the voice of the customer avenues and listening posts. Customers represent different areas of emphasis and levels of profits that are important for different parts of the organizational design. Some customers are highly profitable for the company; others are not so profitable, which makes it necessary for companies to make critical policy decisions, depending on what market segment they should be going after. Therefore, CRM plays an important part in discerning the differences regarding putting into practice what works and what does not work in making market segmentation decisions.

Managing customer relationships represents a cost-effective option for an organization wanting to improve its business results in a direct way and reduces marketing and operation costs. Investments in CRM process changes can be made incrementally and can generate immediate measurable cash flow benefits. CRM performance depends upon the effectiveness of the process and meeting the intent of the organizational value system.

It is very important for any organization to keep abreast of dramatic changes in the marketplace and to collect and store information on trends of customers' wants, needs, and requirements. Therefore, CRM processes must be geared to obtaining data, information, and knowledge on customers' wants, needs, and requirements and on market trends. To be responsive and competitive, CRM must be conducted in a systematic way to capitalize on any golden opportunities as quickly as possible.

A CRM SYSTEM

A CRM system is a set of skills and competencies that enable a company to take better advantage of and more profit from each customer relationship. Although most CRM systems can deliver significant advantages of cost cutting, revenue generation, and customer retention, the task of implementing and maintaining a CRM solution can be overwhelming for any organization. A CRM process, when properly formulated, derives solutions that will help clients to build and to take action on the strategies that assist business managers to work effectively with whatever type of system is implemented. At the end of the day, the CRM process is about seeking good solutions for the organization steeped in customer information. The solutions must include the following:

1. An implementation plan
2. Integration with existing IT infrastructure
3. Analysis and modification of existing systems
4. Post-implementation support after action review
5. Increased customer retention and loyalty data
6. Rapid return on investment strategies
7. Reduced sales cycle methodologies

8. Increased sales and profit centers
9. Improved customer relations planning processes

Customer Culture

Heeding the voice of the customer is the ability to listen and actually hear and determine what the customer wants, needs, or requires, which all boils down to understanding customer culture. Customer culture is about navigating tumultuous changes and building an organization where change is second nature to all those who embrace it. Change is inevitable; one can either be happy by embracing it or miserable by trying to fight it. It all depends upon outlook and attitude.

> *"One cannot manage change. One can only be ahead of it."*
> Peter Drucker,
> *Management Challenges*
> *for the 21st Century*

Customer Commitment

During my visit to Fayetteville, Arkansas, for a regional conference, I was fortunate to be able to go on a tour to see the Billionaires' Backyards—Walton, Tyson, Hunt, and Georges. At the first 5&10 Wal-Mart store, established in 1951 in Bentonville, Arkansas, I was able to pick up from the tour guide a copy of "Sam's Rules for Building a Success," now printed in French, German, Spanish, Portuguese, Chinese, Korean, and Japanese. This simple document with 10 simple rules propelled a retail empire—now almost $345 billion and growing. Wal-Mart's global presence in 2007 spans the following countries with low-cost, low-price stores: UK 336 units, China 73 units, Japan 292 units, Canada 289 units, US 4,000 units, Mexico 896 units, Guatemala 133 units, Honduras 41 units, Nicaragua 40 units, El Salvador 63 units, Costa Rica 139 units, Puerto Rico 54 units, Brazil 299 units, and Argentina 14 units, totaling an international operation of

2,700 units and 4,000 domestic U.S. units. All these stores have a motto: "Everyday low cost equals everyday low price." Their accomplishment relies on Sam's 10 rules of success:

1. Commitment to business
2. Sharing with associates and partners
3. Motivating employees
4. Communicating everything
5. Appreciation of everything
6. Celebrating associate success
7. Listening to everyone
8. Exceeding customers' expectations
9. Controlling costs
10. Swimming upstream against the conventional wisdom

People often ask, "What is Wal-Mart's secret to success?" In response to these questions Sam Walton in his 1992 book *Made in America* compiled a list of 10 key factors that unlock this mystery. These factors, known as "Sam's Rules for Building a Success," contain the following:

Sam Walton's Rules of Success

- Rule 1: COMMIT to your business. Believe in it more than anybody else. I think I overcame every one of my personal shortcomings by the sheer passion I brought to my work. I don't know if you're born with this kind of passion or if you can learn it. But I do know you need it. If you love your work, you'll be out there every day trying to do it the best you possibly can, and pretty soon everybody around will catch the passion from you—like a fever.
- Rule 2: SHARE your profits with all your associates, and treat them as partners. In turn, they will treat you as a partner, and together you will all perform beyond your wildest expectations. Remain a corporation and retain control if you

like, but behave as a servant leader in a partnership. Encourage your associates to hold a stake in the company. Offer discounted stock, and grant them stock for their retirement. It's the single best thing we ever did.

- Rule 3: MOTIVATE your partners. Money and ownership alone aren't enough. Constantly, say by day, think of new and more interesting ways to motivate and challenge your partners. Set high goals, encourage competition and then keep score. Make bets with outrageous payoffs. If things get stale, cross-pollinate; have managers switch jobs with one another to stay challenged. Keep everybody guessing as to what your next trick is going to be. Don't become too predictable.

- Rule 4: COMMUNICATE everything you possibly can to your partners. The more they know, the more they will understand. The more they understand, the more they'll care. Once they care, there's no stopping them. If you don't trust your associates to know what's going on, they'll know you don't really consider them partners. Information is power, and the gain you get from empowering your associates more than offsets the risk of informing your competitors.

- Rule 5: APPRECIATE everything your associates do for the business. A paycheck and a stock option will buy one kind of loyalty. But all of us like to be told how much somebody appreciates what we do for them. We like to hear it often, and especially when we have done something we're really proud of. Nothing else can quite substitute for a few well-chosen well-timed, sincere words of praise. They're absolutely free—and worth a fortune.

- Rule 6: CELEBRATE your success. Find some humor in your failures. Don't take yourself so seriously. Loosen up, and everybody around you will loosen up. Have fun. Show enthusiasm—always. When all else fails, put on a costume and sing a silly song. Then make everybody else sing with you. Don't do a hula on Wall Street. It's been done. Think up your own stunt. All of this is more important, and more fun, than you think, and it really fools the competition. "Why should we take those cornballs at Wal-Mart seriously?"

- Rule 7: LISTEN to everyone in your company. And figure out ways to get them talking. The folks on the front lines—the ones who actually talk to customers—are the only ones who really know what's going on out there. You'd better find out what they know. This really is what talking quality is all about. To push responsibility down in your organization and to force good ideas to bubble up within it, you must listen to what your associates are trying to tell you.

- Rule 8: EXCEED your customers' expectations. If you do, they'll come back over and over. Give them what they want—and a little more. Let them know you appreciate them. Make good on all your mistakes, and don't make excuses—apologize. Stand behind everything you do. The two most important words I ever wrote were on the first Wal-Mart sign: "Satisfaction Guaranteed." They are still up there and they have made all the difference.

- Rule 9: CONTROL your expenses better than your competition. This is where you can always find the competitive advantage. For twenty-five years running—long before Wal-Mart was known as the nation's largest retailer—we ranked number one in our industry for the lowest ratio of expenses to sales. You can make a lot of different mistakes and still recover if you run an efficient operation. Or you can be brilliant and still go out of business if you're too inefficient.

- Rule 10: SWIM upstream. Go the other way. Ignore the conventional wisdom. If everybody else is doing it one way, there's a good chance you can find your niche by going in exactly the opposite direction. But be prepared for a lot of folks to wave you down and tell you you're headed the wrong way. I guess in all my years, what I heard more often than anything was: "a town of less than 50,000 population cannot support a discount store for very long."

CUSTOMER VALUE ANALYSIS

Positioning your organization for success depends on finding what your competitive advantage is. One way to find this out is by performing a customer value analysis (CVA). There are several consultants in the market that can provide the services and the software to do this job for you. One of the better known ones is Zytec Industry. CVA is in knowing your competitive position through the voice of the market—that is, getting better market data. Sometimes the value gained from a fairly modest amount of required data to assess the relative customer-perceived value of different brands is just as good.

However, a fair value line can be determined by first charting a value map. The value map is an invaluable tool for tracking how customers perceive your products.

> **The Value Map displays the benefit-versus-price choice that your customers face as they evaluate your products against competitors. Armed with a carefully developed Value Map, managers can see instantly how competitive their products are. In companies that do a good job of managing customer value, managers at all levels use Value Maps to track how their customers perceive them in a world in which competitors' prices, products and features are continuously changing.**[1]

Whether your customers happen to be households or businesses, they all look for products that give them the best value for their money. This is what drives value perceptions. The CVA works best when the customer has a high degree of customer choice with a more cognitive approach than effective approaches such as in business to business. Quality and price are equated to value on the value map.

Obviously, the path to improved customer value begins with data, which provides the answers to the following sets of questions:

1. What do your customers want?
2. Which suppliers are performing well or poorly against these wants?

3. Do you offer customers good value relative to your competitors?
4. How much are your products are really worth?
5. What improvements to your product would be worth the most to customers?
6. How do you set prices to be competitive?
7. How do you capture the full worth of your product?
8. How do customers view your product or services with the role of marketing communications?
9. How do customers perceive your brand?

The market profile is all that is needed to begin analyzing customer value. Data is typically gathered from market research and competitive intelligence. Surprisingly, some of the above questions can be answered with a fairly modest amount of data required to assess the relative customer-perceived value of different brands. You are likely to have most of the data you need already in your files. You can put together a best-guess estimate for the data based on your management team's knowledge of the market. Building "mental models" is another first step to gathering data, which can be analyzed with research-based data. All this staging helps to identify areas where management misperceptions might be leading the business in the wrong direction.

NOTE

1. http://www.cval.com/cva.htm.

CHAPTER

Customer Focus

> *"The approach that gives you the best shot of taking care of the customer is the same one that best takes care of you."*
>
> Price Pritchett

CUSTOMER SUCCESS BY CREATING A WORLD-CLASS OPERATION

An organization can achieve customer success using quality tools through creating a world-class operation. In Chapter 4 the process levels of change show how to get to customer success, which is the highest level of catering to the customer's wants, needs, or requirements. World-class organizations must understand what a customer-focused organization is and exactly what customer focus means.

The new paradigm of world class to meet competitiveness for companies is customer focus. To better understand this new emerging phenomenon, know that customer focus is achievable for both internal and external customers. The three areas of customer focus are:

1. Customer satisfaction
2. Customer delight
3. Customer success

THE THREE CUSTOMER PARADIGMS

The customer satisfaction paradigm is where customer expectations are known as *critical-to-customer satisfactions*. At this stage there is also a requirement known as *critical-to-customer requirements*. The customer delight paradigm, where moments of magic almost always happen, is first achieved through exceeding customer expectations to provide one plus more to reach the customer success paradigm. In these three paradigms, part of the ideal state of customer satisfaction becomes the moment of truth. Once an organization reaches the could-be platform, it is at the beginning stage of an organization becoming "good." To reach the customer delight paradigm, there is another occurrence, which is the moment of magic. The organization will first pass through the moment of magic meeting the specifications (the customer satisfaction paradigm) before it ascends to meet or exceed customer expectations at two different stages, the moment of truth (good) to the moment of magic (excellence). Only then will the organization reach the one-plus-more stage, which is outstanding (great).

After succeeding to the customer delight paradigm, an organization must continue to be outstanding by providing one-plus-more levels of performance. When an organization arrives at this state, it is in the customer success paradigm reaching for greatness. Figures 7.1 and 7.2 graphically depict these conditions.

CUSTOMER SATISFACTION PARADIGM

The customer satisfaction paradigm is when an organization finally has matured and reached the threshold of high performance, the beginning stage to become a world-class operation. This is the moment of truth. The organization has achieved the specification level of satisfying the customer or meeting what was promised, and the organization is waiting to launch itself from good to great. When an organization begins to understand the why, what, and how of high-level performance, it is ready,

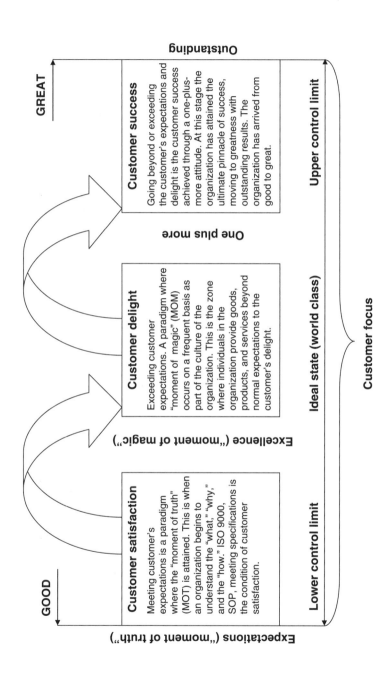

Figure 7.1 Customer focus paradigm

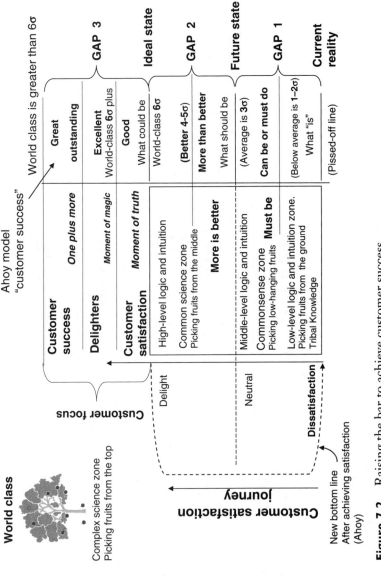

Figure 7.2 Raising the bar to achieve customer success

willing, and able to position itself to launch into the Lean and Six Sigma methodologies. Process improvement in the DMAIC (define, measure, analyze, improve, and control) mode brings the existing process capability to the moment-of-truth level through common science solutions and new processes though the one-plus-more level that is achieved through the design for Six Sigma mode, which is the complex science zone. To promote an organization beyond the Six Sigma level, the TRIZ methodology must be in place (see Chapter 11).

CUSTOMER DELIGHT PARADIGM

The customer delight paradigm, where moments of magic occur on a frequent basis as part of the culture of the organization, is derived through solutions provided by knowledge-based workers who impart the core value propositions of the organization. At this level, an organization has knowledge-based workers who have moved from stages one, two, and three to the stage four level of change needed to achieve this position.

CUSTOMER SUCCESS PARADIGM—ONE PLUS MORE

Customer success is not just customer satisfaction. Instead of merely meeting customer satisfaction, those aspiring to become a world-class company must understand the voice of the customer with a new appreciation of customer experience beyond satisfaction. The new mantra is customer success through creating a world-class operation. To reach the lofty goal of achieving customer success, an organization must build good relationships with its existing customer base and develop potential customers by having the right people with the right attitude in the right place in the organization. It is about looking at the organization from its as-is condition to its must-be condition to reach the future state, then on to more than better, and the could-be platform of customer satisfaction. The moment of truth (meeting customer expectations) is only the beginning of the ideal state of customer delight—moments of magic (meeting or exceeding customer expectations)—before finally reaching the customer success paradigm of one plus more. All three—customer satisfaction, customer delight, and customer success—are in the ideal state or the world-class realm. Figures 7.1 and 7.2 show the levels of transformation involved in moving operational excellence upward, necessarily filling the gaps to become effective.

The customer success attitude requires empowering employees with a one-plus-more mentality to perform outstanding results. Employees in a corporation or in the private, not-for-profit sector are constantly drilled on implementing customer satisfaction (moments of truth) and customer delight (moments of magic). Delivering goods, products, and services with a one-plus-more paradigm is the way of the future to put an organization at the high-performance level of the customer success paradigm. This one-plus-more initiative is a mantra that is practiced by the most aggressive, forward-looking organizations. Customers generally get to expect three levels of experience from a world-class operation: a moment of truth, a moment of magic, and the one-plus-more phenomenon in every successive transaction. There are different performance interactions with different organizations.

DIFFERENT PERFORMANCE INTERACTIONS

Customer success is the highest form of customer focus and requires a different level of interaction to change the way providers achieve their goals, retain their market share, and grow. Every organization needs to excel in providing goods, products, and services, better, cheaper, and faster. Therefore, they must transform their organization from the *surviving* mode to a *thriving* mode. They must learn to improve their processes through high-level relationship building and to create an effective organization with operational excellence in everything they do.

An effective organization becomes leading edge and ready to compete with the best of the best. In these tumultuous times of rapid changes in a global economy, there is no room for error. There is no second chance; your competition will fill in the void if you create one or miss your place. To reach a level of performance that reaches global competitiveness means doing the right things right the first time and for a long time thereafter. The aspiration of any enterprise to create a world-class organization requires a tactical and strategic viewpoint, followed by a short term with much longer-range preparations, and an extended vision.

BEYOND NORMAL SERVICE

> *"Quality is doing the job right every time, but perfection is doing the right job right every time."*
>
> Christopher Ahoy,
> Lectures–Creating Awareness
> for World-Class Operations, 1997

It is necessary to go beyond normal service to be outstanding and ultimately to achieve customer success. You shortchange yourself, your coworkers, and your customers by merely providing customer service satisfaction. Customer success is the new mantra where quality is doing the job right every time, and perfection is doing the *right job right* every time. What most people do not realize is that superior customer service skills add to every area of life because they help to build superior relationship skills.

This reminds me of when President Kennedy was asked if he would be the vice presidential candidate with Johnson as the presidential candidate. He said, "Why take the second position when you have an opportunity to go for the top position?" Customer success places the customer experience in the forefront of any discourse. Superior relationship building is a necessary ingredient for customer success. The success of the customer is paramount in a relationship that also results in long-lasting benefits to the provider.

CLEARLY FOCUSING ON CUSTOMER SUCCESS

Organizations must clearly define what is needed to create customer success. They must teach their employees that customer success really is accomplished by sharing success stories. One such example that comes to mind is of a sales clerk making an extra effort to help a customer understand why the clerk was not able to change a coat that she had bought the previous day. In this particular incident, the customer after returning home felt that the coat was a little large. The next day she returned to the shop to exchange the coat, but none of the other coats on the rack would fit. The sales clerk asked the customer to accompany her to the office while she telephoned other stores around the country to find her exact size. After several hours of trying, the sales clerk was unsuccessful. However, since the customer still liked the coat that she had purchased the previous day, and seeing the extraordinary effort the sales clerk had made to satisfy her, she decided that she would keep the coat. Instead of asking for her money back, she went home satisfied. She happily leaves the premises with a slightly oversized coat—truly a moment of magical customer experience!

With the need to cater to similar requirements for customer experiences, more enlightened companies are spending a lot of time, energy, and money today on customer relations management. Why is customer success so important now? Why is it the highest level of service performance? Any organization hoping to beat its competition must be a value-based organization.[1] This is very well explained in Richard Barrett's book *Building a Values-Driven Organization: A Whole System Approach to Cultural Transformation*. A value-based organization goes beyond fulfilling the customer's wants, needs, and requirements—going beyond the mere satisfaction and excellence of providing outstanding performance.

WHAT IS CUSTOMER SUCCESS?

Customer success is a philosophy of serving a customer or a group of customers. It is beyond customer satisfaction and delight!

For example, when banks loan money to a business enterprise, customer satisfaction normally stops at the point where the borrower secures the loan, and that is the end of the transaction. It is not necessarily the responsibility of the bank to follow up to see how the borrower is managing the funds. In a customer-focused organization and a customer-success environment, the bank would see to the successful enhancement of the business plan presented as part of the loan application process, assuring that the borrower is successful in the endeavor; thus, assuring the security of the loan as well. The bank thereby benefits by making sure the borrower is successful and thriving. Just observe today's economy where banks made risky loans 20 percent above the home's value, resulting in thousands of foreclosures. Statistically, one cannot project the line of regression into the future.

Similarly, it is not the current practice for a physician to follow through with a patient once he or she is satisfied with a diagnosis, treatment, or cure. In this example, if there were a customer-success focus, the doctor would follow through within a day or week with a phone call to assure the total well-being of the patient. Regardless of the condition of the patient's disposition, the doctor would have put in place the after-the-treatment (cured or not) follow-up to assure that the relationship building is never ending, and that new learning is constantly and continuously applied throughout the life cycle of the individual. This follow-through best practice is applicable to any organization interested in successful outcomes.

In academia the expectation of the process model imposed on the education system is shown by one of the metrics as the number of degrees granted. In this case the customer could be the parent. The successful graduation of the offspring indicates the ability of an institution to confirm capability and capacity to the student. The students' competencies in the fields of their endeavors are the expected outcome. Customer success for the institution could be to follow the welfare of the graduate by maintaining a connection through the alumni association, and not just for soliciting funds.

HOW DO YOU ACHIEVE CUSTOMER SUCCESS?

First, you must look for ways to understand the voice of the customer by building successful relationships. We all know that building relationships is about people. Most customers are looking for an organization that provides for its needs for goods, products, or services, better, cheaper, and faster. You have to have an effective organization well versed in all the functional components to achieve that goal. Effective organizations are those enterprises that are aware that a right process must be put in place to derive operational excellence to meet or exceed customer expectations. Meeting or exceeding customer expectations will lead an organization to provide goods, products, and services to delight the customer. However, the key to achieving customer success is to follow through and keep up long-term relationships.

In Chapter 6, we discussed the need to understand the phenomenon to achieve customer delight. There are basically three stages of organization development needed to achieve this phase of ultimate customer delight and customer success. The initial stage is the mapping of current reality or the "is" state to find what works and what does not work. The second stage is to remove waste through Lean initiatives by using commonsense principles and picking the low-hanging fruits. This is the launching pad or the perceived future state to move upward toward the ideal state where common science and complex science principles and methodologies are required and where the waste is removed and the variation and the defects are minimized. Achieving this stature is arriving at the threshold of being a world-class operation. *To achieve ultimate customer satisfaction is customer success.* The customer success environment can only happen when an organization is humming flawlessly in all its operations with near perfection in its processes and with almost zero defects. World-class attributes and practices are well placed when customer success traits are fostered and engendered in its employees and when its workforce development is well understood.

THE SEVEN STAGES OF WORKFORCE DEVELOPMENT

Stage I—The Worker Is Unaware and Unskilled

The low level of logic is in the intuition zone (see Figure 3.2). According to the Six Sigma level of expertise, stage one is at the one- and two-sigma levels. That is 668,000 DPMO or 330,000 DPMO. This is the commonsense zone or the low-level logic and intuition level.

Stage 2—The Worker Is Aware and Unskilled

The middle level of logic and intuition is in the Lean zone, capable of removing waste and of creating a flow in the processes as in Lean process improvement. At this stage, workers are at 93.3 percent process yield of a three-sigma level of skill–just average. An organization at this level is also possibly average relative to a world-class operation. Three-sigma is 66,807 DPMO. This is the Lean zone and still in the commonsense zone where the application is concerned with waste elimination and the creation of flow in the process is evident.

Stage 3—The Worker Is Aware and Skilled

The worker is still the middle level of logic and intuition for the knowledge-based worker who has gone through the necessary training and development, and has mastery of his or her area of expertise. This knowledge-based worker has the profound knowledge to tackle problems and issues of existing conditions and to take the appropriate corrective and preventative actions. This is the common science zone, where process optimization occurs. Stage three in the Six Sigma language is the application of DMAIC methodologies.

Stage 4—The Worker Is More Aware and Skilled

The worker is tending toward the high level of logic and intuition where problem solutions are handled at the expert level.

This provides process capability yielding 99.98 percent process yield of four- or five-sigma level performance improvement. Performance capacity is only 6,710 DPMO at four-sigma or 233 DPMO at five-sigma. When workers reach this level of expertise, we call it arriving at the threshold of coming close to a world-class operation. This is still in the common science zone, but is now using design of experiments in certain aspects of problem resolution. Knowledge workers at the fourth and the fifth stage of development are highly prized and sought after by leading-edge companies to populate their pool of very talented workers. These are the stalwarts of industry, capable of producing very high-level performance consistently with unbiased, repeatable metrics to create customer success.

Stage 5—The Worker Is a Highly Trained Black Belt

He or she is automatically performing high-level work with tacit knowledge. This is an individual who is focused and skilled and is in the highest state, the highest level of logic and intuition. This knowledge-based worker has gone through the necessary training and development, has mastery of his or her area of expertise, and possesses profound knowledge with the ability to tackle problems and issues of existing conditions–including those of the future when designing the future state, taking the appropriate corrective and preventative actions. This individual through creation and re-creation of processes is able to reduce variance and check for mistakes. At this level of expertise the organization is endowed with knowledge workers at their pinnacle of high-level performance. Now, this is the zone of complex science, where process capabilities are tested and designed for the Six Sigma level of performance. In the Six Sigma language, a stage five application is the design of experiment and design for Six Sigma methodologies. On the scale of defect occurrence, it is a mere 3.4 DPMO, still the baseline of a good organization positioning itself to be a great organization. Knowledge workers at this stage are cognizant of the customer success paradigm.

Stage 6—The Worker Is Highly Creative, but Not Differentiating

This area of expertise normally has been relegated to inventors who come up with new goods, products, and services. At this level the paradigm is achieving a scale beyond the Six Sigma level of performance. Although the process may involve looking at stages 1, 2, 3, 4, 5, and 6 levels of solutions before achieving analyses extracted from answering questions at each step of these stages, the final outcome is derivative and is inspirational, and discovery is through a new paradigm shift.

Stage 7—The Worker Is Highly Creative and Differentiating

This worker is on a spiritual journey, ascending beyond information and with knowledge bordering on extreme wisdom potential (see Figure 2.2). This is the ultimate, the zone of greatness for an organization where outstanding results are achieved. It is where any organization will be achieving the customer-success level and giving the one-plus-more level of service. Knowledge workers with development are revered as sages.

WHAT ARE THE CHALLENGES?

What are the challenges facing each organization aspiring to attain world-class status? If you look around your own business, the prime directive appears to be customer satisfaction. Customer satisfaction is not enough in this multicultural age. The new mantra is customer success. You literally have to provide a full range of services from beginning to end and keep in contact with your customer with follow-ups. This is a point-and-click societal era, and the demand for future services for customer success beyond customer satisfaction and delight is what is needed, including a full range of services and customer experiences to make customers successful in their own enterprises. In other words, if you want to gain customer loyalty and create a lifetime-repeat customer, then provide a full service package from cradle to grave, or womb to tomb or even better, cradle to cradle, sometimes referred to also as womb-to-womb services and then some.

If your customer is successful, your organization will also be successful and will reap bountiful benefits in the form of greater wealth in every way, including goodwill and monetary gains endowed with long-lasting relationships. If we want repeat, loyal customers and wish to discourage them from seeking other avenues to fulfill their expectations, it does not take a rocket scientist to tell us that we better find a way to fulfill the voice of the customer. It is not enough to merely greet them and sell them goods, products, and services without understanding their business and the urgency they feel to fulfill their expectations.

Training and development of human resources are required to create operational excellence and reach organizational effectiveness. You have to do the following:

- Fulfill the voice of the customer and the voice of the employee.
- Look at the entire organizational excellence from a systems perspective.
- Fill in the gaps through gap analyses.

There is a challenge to develop high-level relationship building by focusing on process and not on task. Training and development of human resources are required to create the operational excellence needed to reach organizational effectiveness. An organization must assess, evaluate, and promote core competencies for its employees to attain world-class capacity and capability. If one aspires to become world class, this requires an innate, thorough understanding of the three cycles of life to determine what an organization needs to do with its systemic and humanistic resources. Superior relationship building is the order of the day for world-class operatives; relationship building requires the right kinds of skills.

Superior Relationships

Relationship building requires the right kinds of skills. A superior relationship is a long-term mutual relationship that is beneficial to both parties. Long-term relationship building requires the right kinds of skills developed through operational excellence and effective organization. These relationships between customer and provider are also directed toward reaching the pinnacle of success. Relationship building is a science and an art form that requires having the right people in the right place interacting with both suppliers and customers. It follows, therefore, that employees must have core values, a strategy, and communication skills that exhibit enthusiasm and motivation. Enthusiasm and motivation evolve when employees experience growth through building self-equity and organizational equity. They will experience success through superior customer relationships and will develop outstanding customer experiences.

> *"Superior relationship building is the order of the day for world-class operatives; relationship building requires the right kinds of skills."*
>
> Christopher Ahoy,
> Lectures—Creating Awareness for
> World-Class Operations, 1997

A good personal relationship, especially long term, is the key to any business or human success development. For instance, more firms are returning to real live voice connections for customer telephone inquiries. Instead of the digital answering machine, requiring one to jump through many hoops, the live service representative assures that the customer's inquiries are satisfied. Digital answering machines just cannot be programmed to anticipate all customer needs. Even speaking to a live person who does not have the same cultural background can be frustrating. Therefore, organizations must clearly focus on customer success through training employees to understand the sensitive paradigm of sales interaction.

EMPLOYEES AND THE ORGANIZATION

Customer success relies on bringing employees and the organization into sync with world-class operatives and with appropriately measuring progress. Critical choices are important using the appropriate quality toolkits for internal and external process improvements. Achieving customer success requires developing world-class operatives in three areas of focus–business, operation, and process. This is accomplished through organization design, through process improvements, and by tweaking the organization's intellectual capital. Intellectual capital includes people, processes, and place of operation. Any changes applied must be evolutionary and not revolutionary to build a solid foundation for future growth.

PROCESS IMPROVEMENTS

Customer success involves process improvements. Customer success enterprises must look at their processes, and decide how to go about making improvements. Process improvement is the third leg of the stool for continuous improvement through various quality initiatives. These improvements, removing waste and variation, can be accomplished by using Lean and Six Sigma methodologies.

Reliable Workflow

Customer success enterprises must have an uninterrupted flow of their goods, products, and services to meet or exceed the customer's expectations. Therefore, there must be a reliable workflow devoid of waste and process flaws. A philosophy of using the right tools to solve problems is part of the customer-success focus. The prime directive for any successful enterprise involves making sure not only that its own processes have a smooth uninterrupted work-in-progress flow, but that its customers' processes are part of this equation. This can be accomplished by using a number of harmonious quality tools to achieve organizational effectiveness and operational excellence, which builds long-term customer relations.

World-class processes are about reliable workflow. This is the new wave methodology through process management for successful operations of high performance. It is developing operations within your organization to achieve customer satisfaction and, ultimately, customer success by establishing a long-term relationship that is mutually beneficial. It is not about making profit for the sake of profit. It is making sure that all parts of an enterprise, the supplier, input, process, output, and customer (SIPOC) are healthy. Those who contribute to the success of an enterprise are part of the total equation. A holistic approach to a win-win situation is better than a win-lose operative. We know that the sum is greater than each of its parts and the noble and moral notions that "we are all created equal with certain inalienable rights to life, liberty, and the pursuit of happiness" are of utmost importance. We are all in this universe together, and none of us can exist without the others. We are interdependent. Civilization is about creating useful and effective organizations for the good of all concerned if we are to live together peacefully on planet earth and be successful through good practices.

INCULCATING CUSTOMER SUCCESS

Many companies should be inculcating a customer-success attitude and vital behavior modification into their organizations. The differentiation of customer success and customer satisfaction is in the current methodology practiced by most enterprises that have been "doing things right" instead of seeking new questions and answers regarding doing the "right things." Continuing to do business as usual because it has always been done that way will not sustain us in the future. Organizations must be moving from a survival mode to a thriving mode to be the best of the best, producing outstanding results to achieve customer success. If an organization is to have a competitive advantage in this world of globalization, it must move from the customer satisfaction mode to delighting customers and then going beyond to the customer success modus operandi. This involves moving an organization from the threshold of world-class operatives to the point of being good and passing from good to excellent to great while creating, maintaining, and sustaining outstanding high-level performance.

ENVIRONMENT FOR CUSTOMER SUCCESS

A learning-and-teaching environment must be in place to promote world-class concepts in any organization such that continuous and never-ending quality initiatives and quality improvements (CANEQIAI) become characteristic and deployed systematically throughout the entire organization. The following points need to be understood, and certain actions need to occur for the learning and teaching environment to foster world-class operatives for customer success:

1. Superior high-level performance depends on superior learning.
2. People are born with intrinsic motivation—self-esteem, dignity, curiosity, and joy in learning.
3. Harness the collective genius of people in the organization, and find a home for individual innate talents to grow in a field of opportunities.
4. Focus on the "generative learning" mode to be sure that system thinking precepts are applied to the entire organizational modus operandi.
5. In the face of fierce competition, continuously explore new business and organizational opportunities to create new potential and new sources of sustained growth.
6. Educate customers on total quality "fitness to standard," making goods, products, and services reliable.
7. Promote the philosophy of leaving a place better than you found it and leaving a legacy for others to follow.

"A learning and teaching environment needs to be in place to promote world-class concepts."

Christopher Ahoy,
Lectures—Creating Awareness for
World-Class Operations, 1997

KNOWING THE BUSINESS OF YOUR CUSTOMER

Knowing the business of your customer is very important because only if you know what your customers need and require will you be able to supply them with the critical-to-quality products and services according to their schedules and demands. At times, your organization may have to know the business of your customers, perhaps even better than the customers, to assist them in the journey to success. You must show them how to do it. As the Chinese proverb says, "Give a man a fish and he will live for a day. Teach a man how to fish and he will live for a lifetime."

"Only companies that strive to be the best and to out-perform all others have a hope of surviving in a world where everyone else is trying to do the same."

Hewlett Packard company statement

Customer success is about helping your customers not only to be satisfied with the goods, products, and services at high quality, least cost, and fast delivery—better, cheaper, faster—but you must assure that their very survival and their successes are intractably woven and tied to your operations—perhaps to your surviving and thriving operations.

CUSTOMER SUCCESS BY RAISING THE BAR FOR OPERATIONAL EXCELLENCE

The different levels designed to achieve customer success are shown on the right side of the diagram in Figure 7.2 where there are three gaps to be filled. The gaps include the current reality, the future state, and the ideal state. Current reality begins with the "is" condition, (what is required to move off the bottom line or the "pISsed-off line" is around one or two sigma). Moving to what must be in order to reach the should-be level, the organization reaches a three-sigma level. *This is just average.*

The current reality is the commonsense zone where low-level logic and intuition reside, which is generally the area where one is picking the low-hanging fruits. The future state is the common science zone where the organization has matured enough to use middle-level logic and intuition. At this juncture, the organization is picking the fruits from the middle of the knowledge tree. This is valued at the four- or five-sigma level of improvement. The could-be bar is the platform that leverages the organization for moving into world-class stature from good to great. At this level of "good" the organization is in the beginning stages of customer satisfaction and is moving to customer delight and finally to customer success, which is outstanding and at the level of "great." The ideal state is the final stage, the complex science zone, where the fruit on the top of the tree is the sweetest. Both the common science and complex science zones require simple and complex math to help provide solutions for problems. The use of statistics and design of experiments permeate the top level of high-performance measures.

Statistics provide the understanding and meaning to the data as the knowledge worker begins to define, measure, analyze, improve, and control (DMAIC) existing processes and to create new processes though design for Six Sigma (DFSS). To continue to sustain world-class stature at the "great level," an organization must produce goods, products, and services that are outstanding. This is where the Theory of Inventive Problem Solving comes into play. This theory is briefly described in Chapter 11. The TRIZ methodology of problem solving also comes into play to derive solutions that are beyond Six Sigma quality measures.

RAISING THE BAR

Raising the bar for any organization means achieving operational excellence to create an effective organization. Operational excellence is attained through a higher level of performance improvements at the three levels of administration: business, operational, and process. By moving the bar up from the minimum conditions of the current reality state of the as-is stage, we move on through the must-be or must-do situation, to the should-be condition, which is the future state.

The future state is the perceived position before the more-than-better stage. We then go past the could-be platform condition, which is past the customer-satisfaction stage, to reach the customer-delight stage paradigm. This is the could-be condition platform and the starting point of the ideal state. These are graphically shown in Figure 7.2. Once we reach the low end of the ideal state position, we are at the starting point of the could-be condition of the organization, which is also known as arriving at being good.

FILLING IN THE GAPS

The crux of attaining world-class operatives for any organization is filling in the gaps, which is discussed in Chapter 10. Figure 7.2 shows that there are three major gaps that exist in any organization as it moves up the ladder of evolution from the "is" condition or current reality state in pursuit of performance excellence to become an outstanding organization. Gaps that exist in any organization need to be filled through organization design, by building self-equity for its workers and organization equity through the creation of knowledge-based workers. We need to measure progress through appropriate metrics (see Chapter 9), "measuring what matters," and using appropriate quality tools (see Chapter 11) to effect changes and to implement continuous and never-ending quality initiatives and process improvements.

> *"Find a need and fill it."*
>
> Kaiser Cement Corporation

Problems and issues that arise can be mitigated through gap analyses. These are organizational issues that can be ascertained from gaps of the differences between the current reality state and the future state. Also higher-level gaps are determined from the differences between the ideal state and the future state. Then we must move upward past excellence on to filling the gaps for becoming an outstanding organization that caters toward customer success. Resolving these gaps will help us to reach the customer satisfaction and customer delight paradigm, eventually reaching beyond this position to the customer success paradigm—the ultimate outstanding level of world-class achievement. Sustaining this level of operatives will become a necessary process in order to maintain this highly elevated level of performance expectations for any world-class organization.

NOTE

1. Richard Barrett, *Building a Values-Driven Organization: A Whole System Approach to Cultural Transformation*, Elsevier/ Butterworth-Heinemann, 2006.

Organization Design

> "*Organizations must be mission-focused, values-based, and demographics-driven*"
>
> Frances Hesselbein

Organization design is a methodology used to attain self-equity for employees and then organizational equity. This can be accomplished by using the tool of the Malcolm Baldrige seven categories of management systems for a world-class organization as we did at FP&M.

> "*To reach the ideal state of a world-class operation, transformation of an organization must take place by creating knowledge-based workers and an organization design.*"
>
> Ahoy, Seminars—Creating
> Awareness for a
> World-Class Operation, 1997

Organization design must be a deliberate, conscious, and planned effort with a long-term commitment. In our case we used our 12-year quality journey as our marker. It is the natural outgrowth of three areas of influence: (1) the coping with or managing environmental factors; (2) the resolution of strengths, weaknesses, opportunities, and threats (SWOTs) that an organization faces; and (3) the understanding and nurturing of the unique, cultural, and personal values of the employees. All three areas of environmental factors, SWOTs, and personal values produce a matching process relative to the position that each organization attains to create strategic decisions for the organization (see Figure 5.10).

COPING WITH OR MANAGING ENVIRONMENTAL FACTORS

The environment has a tremendous impact on the socioeconomic conditions of a state or nation. Some of these issues transcend boundaries beyond the control of an individual or an organization. Nevertheless, one must understand the situation, anticipate the currents, and deal with the environment as it impacts the world and the nation, noting how the impacts trickle down to the state, the organization, and finally, the individual level. In our organization design, we must manage and cope with all the environmental factors.

STRENGTHS, WEAKNESSES, OPPORTUNITIES, AND THREATS

Most business organizations do a SWOT analysis during the strategic planning process to understand their strengths and weaknesses by looking at the opportunities and threats that the enterprise may face from external competition or lack of internal progress. SWOT processes assist organizations to carve out a sustainable market niche. If used on the individual level, SWOT helps to assess the individual's career by taking the best advantage of talents, abilities, and opportunities. SWOT analysis helps you to focus on your strengths and minimize threats and take the greatest possible advantage of available opportunities. Some possible questions we need to ask in each of the four categories are:

1. Strengths—What do we do well? What resources can we draw on? How do others see our strengths? How do we see our strengths?
2. Weaknesses—What can we improve? Do we have fewer resources than others in a similar industry? How do others see our weaknesses? How do we see our weaknesses?

3. Opportunities—What opportunities are available? What trends can we see to take advantage of? How can we turn our strengths into opportunities? What are our key performance indicators that can differentiate us from others? How can we innovate?
4. Threats—What trends could harm us? What is our competitor doing? To what threats do our weaknesses expose us? How can we change adversity to our advantage?

CULTURAL AND PERSONAL VALUES OF EMPLOYEES

Cultural values and personal values play a significant role in organizational behavior. Here we are talking about cultural and personal norms that impact an organization derived from individual backgrounds—the schools in which they have been educated, the community from where they came, and their spiritual and religious upbringings. These all play a role in employee reactions to situations, especially in the workplace.

Culture results from the successful attempts to adapt to an organization. Culture presents an opportunity to organization members for a shared strategy of survival. When that strategy becomes restricted, it may become destructive to the organization's attempt to make progress. Sometimes, members of an organization or enterprise may comprise individuals known as *culture keepers*, and they may prevent changes from occurring. On the personal level, the unchanging belief patterns that are detrimental to the organization may emanate from the upbringing of the members of the organization.

A good example of this situation was expressed clearly in the classic movie *South Pacific*, where cultural mores clashed with two groups of lovers—one set from different races and another set of the same race but from different societies and countries. The song portrayed that the couples were not born with prejudices but were taught them from childhood. The moral of the story is that personal values may be destructive to individuals and destructive to organization design.

To be in a position to reach world-class stature, various changes must take place in an organization—the culture, personal beliefs, and an innate understanding of environmental factors, beginning at the bottom of the organization and going to the top and also going from the top of the organization down to the bottom. There are three areas of focus in organization levels: business, operations, and process.

Business

The aspirations and hopes of the organization reside in the business area. As someone said, "Where there is not vision, people are unrestrained." You must develop your purpose or mission to find out why your organization exists. Without a purpose there is not a definite direction set for the organization to go forward.

You must start by asking the five most important key questions that Peter F. Drucker developed in finding where leadership should take the organization and in guiding its members. To define the purpose of the organization the following questions will bring some closure:

1. What is your organization's business (mission)?
2. Who are your customers (internal as well as external)?
3. What do your customers consider of value (include VOE and VOC)?
4. What have been your results?
5. What is your plan of action and how do you want to deploy it?

In the next set of key questions include: "What will the future look like if things are running as planned?" The answers will present an image of the organization's aspiration and provide a picture of the future. The soul of an organization is determined by the value that it gradually implants. The question that should be asked is: "For what do we stand?" Then, look at the near-term goal and ask, "What do we want people to focus on right now?"

The business or mission of a for-profit organization is to assure its stakeholders a return on investment and for the not-for-profit organizations it is to make a difference in human lives. In any business (profit or nonprofit) the mission comes first and, in both cases, with customer success. Organizations must exist to make a difference both in the society and in the lives of the individuals. Translating that mission into action is the responsibility of the leadership in an organization.

Operations

At the operations end of the organization is middle management leadership, which will be in charge of working out the details of the mission or the purpose of the organization. How true the expression that the "proof is in the pudding." A question in this area would be to ask: "What do we want to achieve?" So the task for operations is to determine the specifics of what the organization is trying to do; for what purposes does the organization need resources (money, people, and time), and what does it expect to achieve? Leadership in operations is constantly interpreting the policy decisions and identifying the desired results. It is also looking at the results that can be determined by applying certain methodologies and by measuring performance. It is important for any organization to find out what it does well and do more of it, and what it does poorly and stop doing that. This activity has been described in the SWOT analysis.

The leadership in business and operations must revisit the mission every three to five years to decide whether it needs to refocus. Change happens, and to compete in the global arena an organization must test the waters and the winds of change to ascertain customers' wants, needs, and requirements.

A great deal of operations management is focusing on efficiency and effectiveness of processes. Operations management often includes substantial measurement and analysis of internal processes to see if the system is performing according to plan.

The nature of how operations management is carried out in an organization depends very much on the nature of goods, products, or services that the organization provides.

Operations management involves areas such as project planning, quality management, economic decision making, supply chain management, human behavior analysis, operations research, and many other areas important to the organization it serves.

Process

The process end of an organization is where profound knowledge must reside to move and to effect a smooth process operation with minimum defects for goods, products, and services. Workers must be empowered to perform their task and be able to input ideas and practices for continuous process improvements. The legendary Toyota automobile manufacturing has led the way in factories around the globe in process excellence. The result of this favored position is that Toyota has been able to take greater market share steadily every year from its competitors and make more profit and maintain customer loyalty while they gain new customers. All this access to global process excellence results in less inventory and fewer worker hours to produce the highest quality of cars with the minimum of defects.

A process is a series of interrelated activities and events that add value to products or services before the transaction is completed. Since every activity in life is a process and every process has a series of steps, it is possible to map existing conditions and raise the bar for excellence by continuous improvement cycles.

GOOD TO GREAT ORGANIZATIONS

Organizations must move from the survival mode to a thriving modus operandi. Therefore, it is not enough to arrive at the threshold of being a good organization. Organizations reaching the bottom line of a world-class operation, which I call arriving at the "moment of truth," are just *good* organizations. To be a *great* or outstanding organization, each organization must raise its bar in its quality journey to achieve outstanding results, and it must position itself from first being an excellent organization then to being an outstanding one. Reaching excellence is the condition described as reaching the "moment of magic." In most instances an organization can reach this pinnacle with help from using design for Six Sigma methodologies, design of experiments, or the use of complex science principles. However, to surpass conditions of excellence to arrive at the position of being great or outstanding and to provide one-plus-more for products and services, an organization must understand the basic principles of the Theory of Inventive Problem Solving, or TRIZ, described in Chapter 11.

Since our change initiatives at FP&M appeared to be taking place slowly, we invited an external review team to audit our progress. They reported that we appeared to be "patiently implementing" our planned phases and that we were on target. This was good news! Therefore, it seemed appropriate and necessary for us to create a system to manifest the processes even further and to create a methodology for attaining world-class stature.

OUTSTANDING ORGANIZATIONS ADVANCE FROM GOOD TO GREAT

Since many companies worldwide are capable of achieving this position through an e-learning and e-commerce environment, it is not enough to be an excellent organization anymore. The latest technology is available to all those who aspire to have world-class knowledge and to develop knowledge-based workers as business is conducted globally at the "speed of thought." Any organization aspiring to become the best and to go from good to great must be in pursuit of excellence to become outstanding, and a special relationship must be built. An organization must practice organizational effectiveness through operational excellence in its process management and in every area of its control. As the author from *Good to Great*, James Collins, says, "Having the right people on the bus with the right skills, experience, and depth is one of the critical elements." The new workers who will inhabit this world in a world-class organization are the knowledge-based workers of the 21st century. Highly trained, developed, inspired, and empowered workers will become masters of their craft. They will be ready, willing, and able to leap from the traditional comfort zone to mastery of the challenge zone. They will move from uncertainty to the experience of innovation, differentiation, and creativity, also known as the chaos zone, thus achieving status unparalleled by their competitors.

MANAGEMENT CHALLENGES FOR THE 21ST CENTURY

Management challenges for the 21st century will be the issues of a workforce system and of a workplace with workforce generational differences. A whole generation of a new workforce is in the offing. These new-age workers, by using their common sense, common science, and complex science, will produce high-quality goods, products, and services that are outstanding, that is, beyond excellent standards. These workers, according to Peter Senge, imbibe four characteristics of personal mastery:

1. Mental models
2. Shared vision
3. Team learning
4. System thinking

They will find a need and fill the gaps that exist and move the organization through different levels by using gap analysis. Those gap analyses will depend on which rung of the organizational ladder the workforce development originates.

PEOPLE ARE THE GREATEST ASSETS OF AN ORGANIZATION

We keep repeating that people are an organization's greatest assets. Therefore, the organization must discover the talents of its employees and provide them with fields of opportunities to harvest their capabilities and talents. It is about focusing on the strengths and coping with the weaknesses. It is about building great long-term relationships with each other and with customers, suppliers, and other entities. All this is fostered through a learning and teaching environment with openness, trust, mutual respect, and sensitive leadership.

Leaders must understand who they are, know what their organization is about, and know its people. Personal humility and the "know thyself" motto is what a leader must follow. The leader must understand the business innately so that he or she can give elevator speeches along the way to anyone who is willing to listen and partake in the conversation. No matter the circumstances of your staff members, it is a must for you to understand that each one of them will make a difference, that everyone is equipped with a personal conscience and is motivated to do well. Know their names and find out what they do, who their family members are, and what motivates them (what makes them tick). Find pathways. Give the right directions by managing things and leading people to be empowered to become knowledge workers. Move yourself and your organization along the path to become the best.

An organization is as good as the people in it. Therefore, any organization seeking a world-class level of performance must have the right people in the right place, just as it is necessary to have the correct raw materials in a manufacturing sector to produce quality products. Jim Collins, in his book *Good to Great*, says "put the right people on the bus to get a great organization."

PUTTING PEOPLE FIRST

Putting people first is the key to the success of any organization. Basically there are three essentials for any organization that can be identified to differentiate its modus operandi: (1) a leader must remove barriers to help its people achieve great successes; (2) the essence of a continuous improvement for everyone, individual or organization, is embracing *kaizen* to live a quality life; and (3) leadership is about working in gray areas and understanding the diversity of the culture.

The successful management of any organization is the balancing of systemic and humanistic sides of every operation. Putting people first will help to move a good organization to greatness. There are basically three building blocks for any organization to observe and manage:

1. Humanware
2. Software
3. Hardware

Humanware

Humanware is about empowering people in your organization. To create an effective organization with operational excellence, you need the right people in the right jobs. Some of us are placed into positions in life by circumstances and, despite the trials and tribulations of life, make it work. Would it not be better if we could be coached or counseled to the right fit? Human beings are programmed from the time they are born into this world. Wouldn't it be great if we knew the right processes to inculcate into the individual from the cradle?

Software

The intellectual capital of any organization is its people, the brain trust or the software of the organization. It is also the institutional memory and the capacity of its people, the individual and the organizational strengths that, when combined through cross-functional fertilization, produce a well-oiled team working together for the common good.

Hardware

The hardware is the material, methods, machines, and the capability of the organization to produce, providing good tools, equipment, and facilities for their people to do their jobs well. Better tools and the right kinds of tools produce better quality products and services.

A LEADER MUST REMOVE BARRIERS

A leader must remove barriers from pathways, create an open environment, and find fields of opportunities for the "humanware." Therefore, a leader must be tolerant of others' weaknesses and appreciative of their strengths and differences. Putting people first involves more than good deeds. It involves an attitude and a way of life, be it a working life, social life, or home life, which deserves to be constantly improved.

Robert Louis Stevenson had it right when he said, "A person is successful who has lived well, laughed often, and loved much; who has gained the respect of intelligent people and the love of children ... who leaves the world better than he found it; who looked for the best in others and gave the best he had."

It reminds me of the four rules of living that the author of *The Four Agreements*, Don Miguel Ruiz (Amber-Allen 1952, 1997), coined and to which I have added the fifth:

1. Be impeccable with your word.
2. Don't take anything personally.
3. Don't make assumptions.
4. Always do your best.
5. Leave a legacy.

No matter what the circumstances of your staff, you need to understand that each one of them will make a difference, that everyone is equipped with a personal conscience and is motivated to do well. Find pathways; give the right directions by managing things and leading people to be empowered to become knowledge workers; and direct yourself and your organization to become the best.

The first order of business of an organization is to develop its people to become highly productive workers. To develop high-performance workers is to create knowledge workers. These knowledge workers will have mastery over the current state of the organization's business activities. They will, therefore, develop the ability to look into any future state and any ideal state and to improve their self-equity, which automatically translates into organizational equity.

CREATING KNOWLEDGE-BASED WORKERS

Knowledge-based workers are disciplined and understand the world-class operatives at three levels of administration—business, operations, and process. They have the ability to take an organization out of the trough of chaos and through the various stages of change.

> *"The most important, and indeed the truly unique, contribution of management in the 20th century was the fiftyfold increase in the productivity of the manual worker in manufacturing. The most important contribution management needs to make in the 21st century is similarly to increase the productivity of knowledge work and the knowledge worker."*
> Peter Drucker, *Knowledge Work as a System*, 1999

These champions are leaders at all three administrative levels, and they may be compared to being equivalent to the ancient martial art practitioners. They are the current, lean proponents, the kaizen coordinators, the value-streaming facilitators, and surgical teams of master black belt, black belt, green belt, yellow belt, and white belt process owners of their companies. They go after the significant problems and issues, among the trivial many, with laser-like efficiencies. Thereby, they save billions of dollars for their organizations. The knowledge management accumulated by these masters for their organizations is the fact-based, data-driven, and knowledge-based operatives that comprise the institutional memory of the organization.

CREATING A SAFE ENVIRONMENT FOR KNOWLEDGE-BASED WORKERS

Organizations need to begin with the premise that the entire group of employees in their company should aspire to become knowledge workers. Most operations move from a pyramidal structure to a responsive, centered, empowered system when introducing knowledge workers to their organization. Create a safe environment to develop knowledge-based workers. This helps to build a cadre of highly trained employees who may have acquired or who are in the process of acquiring the necessary skill sets to motivate themselves and others (volunteer versus conscripted) in managing things and leading others through a learning and teaching environment.

> *"The creation of an environment where managers are leading, coaching people and managing things has been and will continue to be a difficult one."*
>
> Ahoy, Seminars—Creating Awareness
> for a World-Class Operation, 1997

Knowledge-based workers must work in a flat organization with operational excellence and in a safe environment. By having profound knowledge of their work processes, which are constantly manifested through process management, the management by methods of why they do, what they do, and how they do it, knowledge-based workers have become the new warriors of this century. They must be agile, adaptable, and able to anticipate and cope with the many changes taking place now and in the foreseeable future. Knowledge-based workers will be able to make appropriate choices and take actions to deal with changes, because they will have a thorough understanding of organizational processes.

These highly skilled mechanics are those who are able to stand in two worlds simultaneously. They must have profound knowledge of existing processes, be able to create the future, and have mastery of their destiny by being creative, innovative, agile, and adaptable. They must be able to anticipate and cope with any changes taking place, from the certainty to the uncertainty arena, while moving out of the comfort zone and into the challenge zone (see Chapter 5).

Removing the "silo" mentality in an organization aligns all creativity, competencies, collaboration, credibility, and communication and makes sure alignment goals are achieved. Knowledge-based workers are able to operate cross-functionally and appropriately, at moments without prompting, to provide fact-based, data-driven information to maintain the flow of work in progress, as well as to anticipate the outcome of the work processes, and to meet and heed the voice of the customer, thereby helping to fulfill customer requirements (see Chapter 6).

Knowledge-based workers, workers who are learners and teachers, have the necessary skill sets to motivate themselves and others (volunteer versus conscripted). They respond to the critical-to-customer requirements, critical-to-customer satisfaction, critical-to-quality, and critical-to-cost imperatives to respond to the voice of the customer, which demands better, cheaper, faster; goods, products, and services through evidence-driven, fact-based, data-driven, and knowledge-based information. This philosophy must be emphasized at the three administrative levels in an organization (see Chapter 5). It is what the knowledge-based workers of tomorrow, the new warriors of the next century, must do to make profound changes for the good of an organization. World-class corporations are actively seeking this advantage.

It is an understood phenomenon that any organization is populated by three kinds of people: (1) The first group of employees is "pioneers." The pioneers are self-starting and are motivated, proactive to getting things done. These folks by nature are the "transformers" in an organization. (2) The second group can be categorized as "settlers." The settlers are those employees who are sitting on the fence and going in either direction waiting for instructions. These folks are "transmitters" and have very little motivation to be proactive. (3) The final group, we call the "CAVE"[1] people—an acronym for citizens against virtually everything. Folks in this category can be nonchalant or disenchanted with the not-invented-here philosophy. Although most folks in this group are good people, they just don't see eye-to-eye with any changes taking place and would rather focus on protecting their turf. They are also known as "culture keepers." However, a few folks in this group may be categorized as "terrorists" and may sabotage the organization with pacifism. We knew there would be many naysayers who would be resistant to change. Therefore, at the outset we decided to focus first on our strengths and on the things we do well and then cope with our weaknesses and with the things we do not do well.

FOCUSING ON STRENGTHS AND COPING WITH WEAKNESSES

By establishing a flatter organization and focusing on our strengths and coping with our weaknesses, we are able to stretch our limited resources of people, machines, materials, and methods. By managing things, leading or coaching people, and creating an environment to be the best, we make it possible for all of us to be empowered, knowledge-based workers. In the creation of the learning and teaching environment, we found a home for many of our talented people—allowing their creativity to prosper through unfettered control and autonomy in a field of opportunities. They began to use their individual creativity from their unique personal backgrounds and to bring their unique contributions to our organization and our parent institution, ISU. As product and service demands increased, the empowerment of employees worked in nicely with the environment of budgetary decrements, as we had to provide much more with fewer available resources.

COVENANTAL RELATIONSHIP

Knowledge-based workers operate best in a *covenantal relationship*. In this case it means those who have a solemn agreement in the way they work with the organization. A covenantal relationship is what the knowledge-based workers of tomorrow, who are the new warriors of the next century, must have in order to make profound changes for the good of an organization. These highly skilled mechanics are imbued with profound knowledge of the existing processes and have the ability and capacity to create the future and have mastery of their destiny. By being creative, innovative, agile, adaptable, and able to anticipate and cope with any necessary changes taking place, they move from the certainty to the uncertainty arena. They are the ones who are always prepared to meet new challenges. Creating volunteer knowledge workers with a covenantal relationship is the best form of practice.

Creative, knowledgeable, volunteer employees do not need contracts; they do need covenants. Organizational covenantal relationships provide the individual with the freedom to act under controlled autonomy. A covenantal relationship rests its foundation on shared values, as discussed in earlier chapters, where commitment to ideas, issues, values, and goals is used to improve organizational processes, thus giving work its meaning, fulfillment, and satisfaction.

VOLUNTEERS VERSUS CONSCRIPTS

Knowledge-based workers are volunteers who are not conscripted to do what is best. Using principles in a controlled autonomy, management encourages volunteerism, creativity, innovation, and differentiation in the production of goods, products, and services in the best interests of the customer. The customer has the right to expect superior quality goods, products, and services at the least possible cost and on-time delivery. At the same time, an enterprise is entitled to produce these goods, products, and services for a profit.

CONTINUOUS QUALITY IMPROVEMENTS

Knowledge-based workers must imbibe the core principles of continuous quality improvement (CQI). This is the prime directive for all operations that are striving to become world class.

However, this in itself is necessary but not sufficient to create an organization that aspires to develop methodologies to create ultimate customer success in the transition from being good to becoming great. We moved ahead at ISU from CQI and coined the acronym CANEQIAI (pronounced "can I") for continuous and never-ending quality initiatives and improvements, which means that CQI is never-ending and is part of our psyche.

Quality Initiatives

Knowledge-based workers are sought after for why they do, what they do, and how they do various operations. They must have occasions and opportunities to show their talents to others and to demonstrate the quality initiatives that have made a difference in their workplaces. The quality initiatives, which we applied at FP&M, have generated outside continuing interests and requests for site visits. These visits have led to additional requests for assistance and information which, in turn, has caused us to improve our "learning and teaching" organization. My staff and I have definitely become better learners and teachers while assisting those seeking information when visiting us. Many visitors inquiring about the implementation of our quality initiatives have gone back with enthusiasm and renewed emphasis for their own journey in moving toward becoming a world-class operation through continuous and never-ending quality initiatives and improvements.

MANAGING THINGS AND LEADING PEOPLE

Knowledge-based workers will be managing things and showing people in their organization how to do the "right things" in contrast to just doing "things right."

This makes it possible for knowledge workers to make a difference by managing things, leading or coaching people, and creating an environment to be the best. In this information age to move forward and be counted in the New Economy, an organization's employees must be trained to become knowledge-based workers, making it possible for all employees in the organization to be empowered workers. It is a necessity that any thriving organization, seeking world-class stature from the outset, gear itself to be a fact-based, data driven, knowledge-based organization, rather than the traditional pyramidal organization in which the staff waits for instructions from above. This transformation is a formidable task for many growing organizations. It is a task, however, in which every organization must be consistent and unrelenting in its pursuit for excellence and high performance.

HIGH-LEVEL PERFORMANCE

Knowledge-based workers are high-level performance individuals. To increase a high level of performance improvement, one must raise the bar of productivity by ascending the learning curve ladder as rapidly as possible. The upward movement from the low-level intuition and logic zone to working with Lean thinking principles takes leadership. Eliminating waste, removing process flaws, defects, non-value-added work, and hidden factories is the next step. Minimizing variance using Lean and Six Sigma methodologies is explained in Chapter 12.

Ultimately, using design for Six Sigma technologies to create new goods, products, and services by asking new questions, demanding better answers, creating future states from current reality to bring about new visions, insights, and innovations results in moving organizations toward the ideal state of world class.

PRODUCTIVITY

> *"Productivity isn't everything, but in the long run it is almost everything. A country's standard of living over time depends almost entirely on its ability to raise output per worker."*
> Paul Krugman, *The Age of Diminished Expectations*, 1994

If you look around in this growing global interdependent economy, the aspiration for any multinational enterprise is to out-produce its competitors in almost everything they do and to gain the largest market share for its goods, products, and services. However, the workers in most organizations are not ready or trained or in the mindset to be positioned to meet the challenges that confront them in terms of productivity based on the work produced by individuals working independently or together. When things go wrong they blame the person rather than the process. Successes or failures of the enterprise depend on the skill, experience, and knowledge, capability, and capacity of the workers and the processes they operate. Hence, any mistaken perspectives may lead to actions and decisions that may adversely affect the standard of the country and the ability of the output of the individual worker.

> *"For real economic miracles you have to look to productivity growth.... In terms of human welfare, there is nothing that matters as much in the long run."*
>
> William Baumol, et al., *Productivity and American Leadership: The Long View*, 1989.

In looking at productivity, enterprises of all sizes are checking their processes to figure the flow and are applying all statistical, technical, and human aspects to learn how they can make improvements. This is the reason why the use of quality tools is so important to achieve high performance.

When an enterprise is able to move to analyzing processes and to rapidly build its workforce to become knowledge-based workers, the defects per quantity of output and the variations in the measurement of productivity are minimized. This could lead an organization to capture its market share sooner than its competitors. Therefore, organizations must:

- Continuously focus on customers' wants, needs, and requirements.
- Improve their mission in serving their customers.

- Achieve a lower productivity cost, a faster response to changing market conditions, and must reach a higher quality.
- Provide a rational methodology for implementing quick changes.
- Reduce waste and inefficiencies.
- Help employees become more productive.
- Create an effective organization with operational excellence.

Work is divided into three parts:

1. Value-added work
2. Non-value-added work
3. Work required by unfunded mandates

Knowledge-based workers are passionately interested in the return on investment, and they focus on optimizing value-added work and on reducing non-value-added work and on operationally non-value-added work with which the customer is not concerned. Therefore, they manage and lead an organization to accomplish an increase in productivity through the production and production capability balance described by Stephen Covey, author of *The Seven Habits of Highly Successful People*

For the organization to survive and succeed in the 21st century, the employee must have fun and find a place where there is purpose, passion, and meaningful work. Therefore, creating knowledge-based workers who are possessed with the skills of creativity, competency, collaboration, and a high level of anticipatory communication becomes a primary and needed function. Organizations, with the right kinds of knowledge workers, gain a competitive edge from the ability of their members to live in the fog of reality and still make quick decisions and excellent interpretations of where the current reality is and where the future state should be in order to reach the ideal state of world-class operations.

NOTE

1. Christopher K. Ahoy, "Leadership in Educational Facilities Administration," APPA 2007 Alexandria, VA, page 138.

Metrics

> *"When you can measure what you are speaking about and express it in numbers, you know something about it. But when you cannot measure it and when you cannot express it in numbers, your knowledge is of a meager and unsatisfactory kind. It may be the beginning of knowledge but you have scarcely in your thoughts advanced to the stage of science."*
>
> Lord Kelvin, British physicist, 1891

I was sitting in a restaurant watching the bartender measuring the quantity of liquor for each drink into the glasses on the tray. The various mixtures exhibited the carefully measured potions. The waitress stood at the counter waiting patiently for the bartender to fill the six glasses. I thought of the number of drinks her customers must have ordered, and how she was keeping tabs for all the refills. Pondering the scene in front of me, I thought of Einstein's profound discovery in quantum physics when he began speculating on the possibility of time standing still. What happens if the clock moved backward or time really did stand still? Who was the first to start measuring; who was the first to invent metrics?

Metrics is prevalent in our lives. Many things that we do in life, we measure. Every day we make thousands of decisions, like how many calories we need to keep the right weight-to-height ratio. We notice how much we weigh each morning as we stand on the bathroom scale. Some of us take blood pressure, diastolic and systolic measurements, to determine how our bodies are responding to our medication or diet. Our well-being depends on our general health, the alignment of our body, mind, and spirit. A few of us may have an Acu-check meter that assures us that the sugar level in our blood is between 85 and 100 mg/dls before breakfast, and that it does not exceed 210 mg/dls after a hearty meal. Others of us might stick a thermometer (Fahrenheit or Centigrade) in our child's mouth to assess whether the child should stay home and recuperate from fever, or go to school.

In our modern-day lives, we are constantly looking at the "dashboard"[1] akin to the dashboard in our automobile to check our speed, the initial and final mileage, brake lights, oil lights, revolution per minute of engine, life of our batteries, and the gas tank level as we make sure all systems are in sync. We are awakened every morning by our alarm clocks. We look at our calendar for the day, month, and year, watch the time in hours, minutes, and seconds. Before we leave the house for work, we check the daily weather conditions. All of these measurements provide some value-added information so we can live our daily lives comfortably and safely.

Many organizations measure too much and acquire more data than is physically or mentally possible to assimilate. Collection of data and data mining may be an impediment to measuring what matters. Data is the alphabetical soup of statistics, and statistics is the scientific answer to what drives a value proposition. While numbers are powerful tools for making better decisions, numbers alone, without the intervention of a human being, do not produce better decisions. Also, the right kind of metrics will determine the process outcome through appropriate key performance indicators for business critical success factors.

The purpose of this chapter is to illustrate what a metric is with respect to what an organization may need to measure in determining how well it is doing in its venture toward becoming world class. Let us look at metrics as one key performance indicator to "measure what matters" in an institution of higher education, specifically in the facilities management area (the list is not all-inclusive):

- Cost Effectiveness—actual project cost as a percentage of budgeted cost
- Staff Productivity—billed hours worked on projects per project FTE (a workload measure)
- Process Efficiency—actual project hours as a percentage of budgeted hours
- Cycle Time—average days to complete a project (by type)
- Percentage of projects completed on time—average time ahead/behind schedule (days) per project
- Drivers—type of project (e.g., size and scheduled duration of project), tenure of project staff, training and certifications for project management, and compensation tied to successful project

CORE METRICS

The development of a core set of metrics for implementing the Balanced Scorecard is the most difficult aspect of an approach. Developing metrics that create the necessary linkages of the operational directives with the strategic mission proves to be fundamentally difficult. It is typical to view organizational performance in terms of outcomes or results, rather than to focus on metrics that address performance drivers that provide feedback concerning day-to-day organizational progress.

Although the metric system is normally used as a measurement based on the meter, here *metrics* is used to name the things that can be measured in order to determine how well we are doing in our day-to-day business operations. The four criteria of the original Balanced Scorecard metrics, or the six criteria of the Balanced Scorecard Plus metrics, are used to determine the appropriate metrics. These criteria are necessary for a data-driven, fact-based, and knowledge-based management operation in order to respond to the critical-to-quality customer needs in producing goods, products, and services that are better, cheaper, and faster than the competition.

MEASURING WHAT MATTERS

To understand whether an operation has made progress, an organization needs to measure what it values. These measurements are the metrics derived for a particular operation. The metrics developed will be specific to each organization and will vary depending on the type of business. However, the key performance indicators that represent the information an organization may need to gauge its improvements can be depicted in the instrument panels (the dashboard) of an operation to monitor the health and well-being of the enterprise. Today dashboards (instrumental panels for monitoring progress) have become management tools. They have moved from the initial phase of modern, graphical, mathematical, statistical adaptation and have become more of a mainstream phenomenon. In a hospital doctors monitor operation processes through sophisticated information technology tools and graphical interfaces—dashboards. Dashboards are being pushed further down the organization hierarchy, from the business level to the operations level to the process level, providing relevant information to "process owners"—supervisors, managers, and division heads—so that they can make informed decisions. Who knows what dashboards will become with data sophistication and nanotechnology?

DASHBOARDS TO SUCCESS

Dashboards to success translate strategies into action. Identify and track key performance indicators as predictive measures for future success. Today many organizations are building dashboard applications that gather and present information for decision makers and knowledge workers at all levels of the organization.

Delivering the data to the dashboard can challenge even the most capable developers of dashboard tools. Data from many different sources must be gathered, integrated, aggregated, and transformed to provide the key metrics. To help decision makers make appropriate choices, the dashboard must be relevant, and metrics must measure what the organization values.

All organizational goals are to be a world-class operation. Conduct a self-study and use a strategy to provide a business plan to the rank and file in the organization. In the strategic planning mode, expect answers to questions derived through the self-study process. Now, how do we make dashboards to success happen? How do we align our employee performance with goals and strategies? And how do we translate strategies into concrete goals and objectives for our organization? These are the challenges facing us in developing a work unit dashboard to success.

Dashboards to success provide the big picture at a glance. They affect the productivity level of workers to deliver goods, products, and services—better, cheaper, and faster through data-driven, fact-based, and knowledge-based operatives. The dashboard provides the mechanism for instant feedback to process owners at different levels in the organization so that they can assess the pulse of their operation and make any necessary changes or improvements.

You have probably heard the old adage a thousand times, "a picture is worth a thousand words." We all want to give our colleagues or staff some mission-critical information in a short time in lieu of a memo or a long written report. You may have been asked to give an "elevator" speech about a pertinent subject and found yourself giving information in five minutes with a few brief explanatory comments and perhaps a graphical diagram that says it all. A dashboard gives instant graphical information.

CREATING A DASHBOARD

Creating a dashboard is complex, but it generally represents a simple graphical presentation of diverse data that can be used to drill down on underlying information. The name came from the dashboards that you are accustomed to seeing inside cars or in an airplane or on any machinery with instrumentation that requires constant monitoring. The cockpit dashboard has various meters that gauge the temperature, check batteries, gas, speed, brakes, direction, wind velocity, altitude, etc. It measures the tachometer speed so the engines and gears are revved up correctly. All are necessary to keep a plane flying safely. An airplane is constantly off course 95 percent of the time, and still the pilot, with the aid of dashboard instrumentation, successfully lands the airplane safely at its destination.

However, the elements of the dashboards to success in an organization are different. These dashboard elements for success can be rearranged, modified, and customized to fit each work unit of an operation. Many can be very simply color coded like the traffic light (red, yellow, or green) to highlight performance known as key performance indicators either above or below expectations.

A red arrow pointing down indicates performance that is below what was expected at that particular point in the project. A green arrow pointing up indicates performance that has surpassed expectations. A yellow arrow pointing to the left or to the right shows performance that has not met some goals but is close to doing so. The use of red, yellow, and green as color indicators of performance is standard to all dashboard presentations. The red color could denote not up to par, the yellow could indicate work in progress, and the green may connote that it is ready to go or that it meets expectations. These are more of the simple type of performance indicators as compared to those with data and graphics.

A dashboard is like a scoreboard. If you were at a basketball game and there was no scoreboard, it would be pretty difficult to assess who won or lost and by how much, let alone allow you to keep track of the ongoing activities. Therefore, a dashboard is a tool used for collecting and reporting data, information and knowledge about vital customer requirements and/or your business performance for key customers. Dashboards provide a quick summary of process, and/or product, or services performance.

Examples of dashboards to success look at cash-flow analyses, budget data sheets, project management or construction management progress sheets, cycle times, work flows, injury rates, training and development, and accounting hits on Web pages, etc. Dashboards to success contain various scorecards in an organization, which are generally known as *performance measures*, populated by instrument panels known as *performance scorecards*.

PERFORMANCE MEASURES

The Performance Scorecard helps an organization set and communicate goals, establish key performance metrics and accountability, and continuously measure performance against organizational goals and objectives. The performance scorecard aligns and focuses on business objectives, plans, and actions. The performance scorecard can empower employees with clearly defined performance measures for success and will enable continuous performance improvement and agility across the entire enterprise.

Superior performance depends on aligning each individual and department in the enterprise with organization strategy and key performance metrics. Performance metrics are key elements of a balanced scorecard. Yet many organizations fail to communicate goals and objectives. And many fail to translate these strategies into meaningful performance metrics that employees understand and for which the employees are accountable.

WHY A BALANCED SCORECARD?

To be competitive and on the leading edge of progress, an enterprise needs the six criteria of the *balanced scorecard plus* components as guidelines for measurement of performance, which lead to operational excellence and an effective world-class organization.

Because lagging indicators mainly consist of financial indicators that measure an organization's past performance and encourage a short-term view of strategy, organizations fail to provide the long-term strategic, process-based management capabilities that they need today. The balanced scorecard was designed to measure organizational performance. Provide appropriate metrics: If you can't measure it, you can't manage it.

KNOW WHEN TO USE A DASHBOARD

Of course, dashboards are not always the best solution for all project status reporting. They are usually aimed at communicating the big picture upstream and across the entire organization, such as the on-time and under-budget statuses of the project. On the other hand, other project management tools can give, in some instances, better task details and functionality in helping to develop, monitor, manage, execute, and predict critical project elements at key points in time. Dashboards can be aimed downstream to individual process owners or upstream from the project manager to the leader. If the goal is to communicate rapidly any data to specific issues or the big picture, dashboards are the way to go. They give you visual communication at a glance in a brief moment.

NOTE

1. Christopher K. Ahoy, "Dashboard to Success," *Facilities News*, Iowa State Facilities Planning and Management, Volume 17, Issue 2, April 2004 (http://www.fpm.iastate.edu/).

CHAPTER

Systems Approach and Filling in the Gaps

> *"There are elements of chance, choice, and certainty in every aspect of our lives."*
>
> Zoroaster, ancient Persian prophet

SYSTEMS ENGINEERING APPROACH

The primary need to create awareness for a world-class operation required that we implement a systems engineering approach to problem solving, using organized creative technologies and methodologies. These organized creative technologies sharpened our definitions and approaches when we looked at the main recurring problems of productivity in our processes. What does an organization do to generate a methodology to take the journey as described to attain world-class stature? Obviously any organization seeking competitiveness and a desire to attain world-class stature must seek an organized creative technology methodological approach to reach its goal. What is organized creative technology?

ORGANIZED CREATIVE TECHNOLOGY

Looking at goal setting, systems synthesis, systems analysis, and the harmony among the quality tools available, we found that the

Baldrige criteria, Balanced Scorecard, and Lean and Six Sigma methodologies appeared to be the most applicable tools for us to use—this was our organized creative technology to move our organization up a notch.

> *"Organized creative technology refers to unified procedures that lie between the initial step or basic research and the terminal operations of manufacture and utilization."*
>
> Arthur D. Hall,
> *A Methodology for Systems Engineering*, 1962

For any organization, moving a notch up means moving out of the comfort zone to uncertainty and changes that lay ahead and moving from doing things right, which had been the modus operandi for most firms, to doing the right things. Because the former condition was comfortable and worked well for what they knew, anything new would be an intrusion into a way of life. Any injection of a new system would be an uncomfortable one that the culture keepers would resist fiercely. What does it take to take an organization up a notch? Your organized creative technology may be slightly different or it may be similar to ours.

SYSTEM THINKING

The power of system thinking is in looking at the totality of a structure like an iceberg where one sees only the tip but there is more to it than meets the eye (see Figure 10.1).

System thinking provides a language for talking about complex interdependencies and can be viewed as follows:

1. Seeing the whole, not just the parts
2. Seeing interdependencies, not just the linear dependencies
3. Optimizing the possibilities and maximizing the potential
4. Looking at the team as "us," not as "them"
5. Thinking in the long term, not just the short term

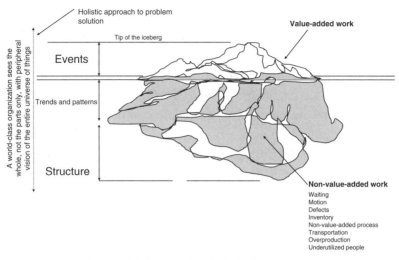

Figure 10.1   System thinking—tip of the iceberg

6. Looking simultaneously at current reality, future state, and ideal state
7. Thinking in levels, not just individual events

> *"System thinking is a conceptual framework, a body of knowledge and tools that has been developed over the past fifty years to make the full patterns clearer and to help us see how to change them effectively."*
>
> Peter M. Senge, *The Fifth Discipline: The Art and Practice of the Learning Organization*, 1990

EVENTS, PATTERNS, AND STRUCTURES

Tweaking the system with small structural changes has a large impact on the total system. Events are like the tip of the iceberg. Trends and patterns are somewhere below the water level. The structure is the solid base. Customers are interested only in the value-added work reflected by the tip of the iceberg. There is a great more happening behind the scenes at the back office to create value to meet the critical-to-customer requirements that are below the surface.

Another way to look at this is to imagine that the iceberg is in the shape of a triangle, where the upper portion of the triangle is the tip of the iceberg (Figure 10.2). Most situations in life follow a pattern where the events are the visible component of the occasion. Trends and patterns occur below the surface when, in fact, the root cause of the problem is not discernable until and unless an organization is able to look deep into the solid foundation of the structure. The structural issue or effect in an organization is deeply rooted at the core, is well hidden, and is not initially perceptible at the surface. Therefore, events are just the tip of the iceberg and do not represent the totality of the system. System thinking, a holistic approach to problem solving, is a must in order for an organization to attain world-class stature.

SYSTEMS MODEL

We must look at an organization from a systems perspective if it is to become world class. We must look at it as holistically developing, drilling down the concepts of a systems approach to organization design, metrics, and process improvements. Knowledge-based workers manage and lead the operation through these precepts and gain a competitive advantage by aligning all of the organization's

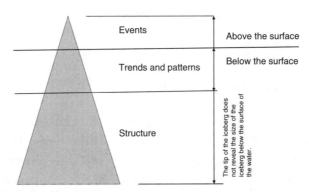

Figure 10.2   Iceberg model (events are just the tip of the iceberg)

activities based on the supply chain model SIPOC (supplier, input, process, output [outcome], and customer).

> *"The organizations that will truly excel in the future will be the organizations that discover how to tap people's commitment and capacity to learn at all levels in an organization."*
>
> Peter M. Senge, *The Fifth Discipline: The Art and Practice of the Learning Organization*, 1990

SIPOC

SIPOC denotes "supplier, input, process, output, and customer." The SIPOC model shows other SIPOC conditions in each of the segments—supplier, process, and customer. Each has its own processes and gaps to fill. However, understanding the customers' wants, needs, and requirements necessitates the ability of organizations to listen to the voice of the customer, which needs to match the voice of the process in order to determine the existing system gaps. The job of every process manager, every operations manager, and every policy level administrator at the business level is to match the voice of the customer with the voice of the process to determine what is value-added work and what is non-value-added work, since the customer is served well by achieving least cost by reducing the latter.

Once the critical to quality wants and needs of the customer are identified through understanding the critical-to-customer requirements, the organization is able to determine critical-to-customer satisfaction. This merely meets the traditional mentality of "meeting the specs" and overlooks the opportunity to reduce costs. If an organization is only responsive to meeting requirements, it will miss the opportunity to reduce costs and to reduce variability around the target value. Mistakeproofing and reducing variability around the target value proposition allows an organization to gain a competitive edge and enables it to produce goods, products, and services, better, cheaper, and faster through fact-based, data-driven, and knowledge-based operatives.

The SIPOC model is a systems model, a holistic way of approaching the entire supply chain value stream until the outcome reaches the customer (Figure 10.3). Each process has subprocesses, as discussed in Chapter 4. Each process also contains within its operations a SIPOC condition (see Figure 10–4). This is important to note since the root cause analysis used to remove defects from subprocesses leads to permanent defect reduction, but this can only be achieved by mapping the current reality. In order to move the operation into the future state or the ideal state condition, each leading and lagging indicator gap must be analyzed and resolved. Variation in each of the output processes causes defects, and defects must be analyzed at every step of the way. This includes any subprocesses in the work flow where there may be issues with variations at the input and output levels.

Though there are many subprocesses within a process, the process management referred to here encompasses a universal, holistic view. We focus on three areas. The first area is an organizational design approach involving creating self-equity and organizational equity—implementing dashboards, using metrics for performance measurement, and using the SIPOC model to remove non-value-added work.

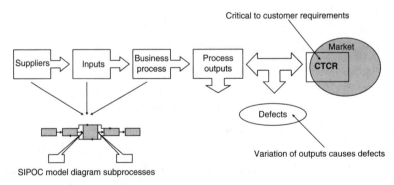

Figure 10.3 SIPOC diagram—supply chain

LEAN SIGMA WAY

In the process model (see Figure 3.5), we stress alignment of work systems by looking at the whole and then at the sum of the parts. In the third area we focus on empowering people in areas of education, leadership style, and developing win-win agreements. All three areas focus on developing a model organization with trustworthiness that helps to perpetuate the Lean Sigma way of operatives.

> *"Quality is the (minimum) loss impact by a product or service on Society."*
>
> Genichi Taguchi

An organization must constantly seek new ways and ask better questions to get better answers. FP&M closed the three gaps using Baldrige, Balanced Scorecard Plus, and the Lean Sigma Way, as well as through the system perspective by using organization design to attain self-equity for employee development of skill sets. This self-equity then translates into organizational equity.

> *If you keep on doing what you've always done, you'll keep on getting what you've always got*
>
> Larry Wilson

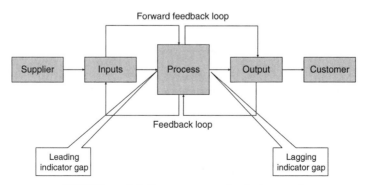

Figure 10.4 SIPOC model diagram—supply chain at subprocesses

GAPS

A gap is defined as an unfilled space or interval—a blank, breaks in continuity, difference, distinction, divergent, disparity, discrepancy, and so on. Chapter 7 covers various gaps that exist in going from the as-is to the must-be (must-do) state—which is the current reality—to the future state, to the more-than-better state, then to the could-be ideal state. The ideal state is the platform where good begins, then on to customer delight, and finally to customer success and greatness. The great ideal state is arriving at the gate of the moment of truth. These gap zones are described in Figure 7.2. The idea is to close each gap shown and to determine what process improvements must take place in order to raise the bar to a higher performance level, achieving excellence in operations for individuals, teams, and organizations. The goal is to achieve a world-class operative existence and to continue to be competitive and a leading-edge organization.

It is necessary to determine gaps in the various levels of administration in the organization for organizational development and to find the necessary bandwidth for incorporating the continuous improvements needed to move to the next level of transformation. To take a work unit's process improvements to the next level, an organization must understand the system perspective of the world-view and the paradigms that restrict or restrain change. The paradigm shift to be incorporated into the organization is explained in Chapter 7. It is only when an organization creates the ability to find the right path, align, and empower its people that it is able to foster an environment of progress that makes it possible for knowledge-based workers to begin to fill the gaps that exist in order to raise the bar for high-performance excellence. The gaps that are occurring in the organization operations at the three levels of administration need to be removed in order to mitigate the difference between where an organization is and where it hopes to go—from its current reality to the future state—before it can attain the ideal state.

Additional gaps (subprocess gaps) that occur within each state will need to be removed to ascertain where the organization hopes to end up. The ideal state is the ultimate goal passed the perceived future state. Gap analyses will show the type of performance required at each level of the organization in order for it to ascend. Data derived from these gaps at the current reality, the future state, and the ideal state provides critical information for developing the building blocks to the future. The future state is where an organization should be to be average! Average is the normal position or platform from which most organizations have the opportunity to reach upward to the ideal state or could-be position. This is world class.

Figure 7.2 shows where gaps exist in each of the three states; the two major gaps are in the learning curve section of the sigmoid curve, with several minor gaps (subprocesses) within the current reality and future state zones. These gaps that exist between the levels of current reality and the future state need to be measured as subsets of the two major gaps. The two major gaps are identified in the process of checking the health of an organization or an individual work unit as it moves up the ladder of transformation. All of these gaps are ascertained by looking at the aspiration of an operation before attaining world-class stature. You must decide which metrics to use in measuring these major and minor gaps at each level described in the learning curve segment of the sigmoid curve.

Gaps in an organization can be measured at the beginning of a process and after the process has been completed (see Figure 10.5 on page 196). The leading indicator gap metrics are at the beginning of process management where the five variables—people, machine, material, method, and environment—are inputted into the processes. The lagging indicator gap is perceived after the process is completed and metrics are established for historical information. Both gap analyses are important to determine the health of the organization. One example of a lagging indicator is the traditional profit and loss statement of a company or organization. Another is the SAT score sheet; both are historical values. However, the best position an organization can take is to ascertain what gaps are being envisaged in the work flow before entering into the process management.

GAP ANALYSIS

Gap analysis is a scientific means for assessing to what extent individuals, teams, and organizations are capable of becoming the leaders of their industry. Organizations positioning themselves to be world class will be the industries of the next century.

To fill these three gaps, analysis is the crux of the resolution to reach customer success. The modified version of the Kano model of customer satisfaction, the Ahoy model of customer success discussed in Chapter 7, provides the solution for attaining a customer success culture. This means moving from the current reality of the as-is condition to the future state of the should-be condition, reaching to the ideal state of the could-be condition or world class. There are three major gaps identified, as we discussed previously. To resolve the analysis of the gap is to move from one condition to another. The differentiation created between where the organization wants to go from where it is, is the goal. The matter to be resolved uses various quality tools to achieve the competitive and leading edge to become a world-class organization.

The goal of gap analysis methodology is first to review the issue at hand by recognizing, defining, measuring, analyzing, and improving processes in the system and, second, is to meet the standards prescribed by the quality initiatives to become world class by measuring what matters. The outcomes from gap analysis are improved processes, processes that are repeatable and measurable. Gap analysis gives process owners at all levels of the organization—employees, supervisors, managers, planners, scientists, and policy makers—the information from data collected that they need to make better-informed decisions when identifying priority areas for organizational change.

Gap analysis emanates from the realization that a unit-by-unit approach to process improvement by itself is not effective because it does not address the alignment of the organization through a systems approach. A systems approach looks at the whole as the sum of its parts and working systems.

Gap analyses must be performed to reach customer satisfaction, customer delight, and finally customer success before attaining the ultimate ideal state of good to great. To achieve customer success we must pass through several zones. The average quadrant, or the zone designated as the low-hanging fruit paradigm, is the aspiration level for many organizations and is the first step before moving ahead to the future state and moving on to the ideal state. The first zone in the level of success attainment is at the three-sigma level of performance as compared to the six-sigma level that is desired to reach the bottom of the ideal state. The six-sigma level is the final zone of success attainment; this, we call the could-be platform at the bottom of the world-class position. It is only when an organization has met all the specifications that it arrives at the moment of truth! This is the "aha!" perception—the "Now I know what it takes to get here."

LEADING AND LAGGING INDICATOR GAPS

There are two categories of measurements used in the Balanced Scorecard. These categories are the leading indicators or performance drivers and the lagging indicators or outcome measures. The performance drivers enable the organization to achieve short-term operational improvements, while the outcome measures provide objective evidence of whether strategic objectives are achieved. The two measures must be used in conjunction with one another to link measurement throughout the organization, thus giving visibility to the organization's progress in achieving strategic goals through process improvement (Figure 10.5).

Some gaps in an organization need to be determined either at the beginning of a process or after the process has been completed. The leading indicator gap metrics at the beginning of the process are most useful from a systems perspective when the

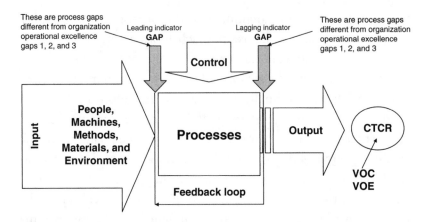

CTCR = critical to customer requirements
VOC = voice of the customer
VOE = voice of the employee

Figure 10.5 System model diagram. The five input variables are people, machines, methods, materials, and environment.

five variables—people, machine, material, method, and environment—are inputted into the processes. The lagging indicator gap metrics at the end of the process are generally used for trend analysis for historical purposes. The system diagram, Figure 10.5, shows graphically the leading and lagging indicator areas. Each of the systems items is described below:

The core control system is a package of integrated component systems for directing and monitoring organizational activities. These components comprise leadership styles (systemic or humanistic or a balance), strategic plans, financial forecasts, budgets, management styles (autocratic, participative, or the "hot" ad hoc approach), management direction (management by doing, management by objectives, operation management techniques, and/or methods described in Chapter 3). Chapter 3 looks at process errors instead of task or personnel errors using evidence-driven, management information, and system reports through fact-based, data-driven, and knowledge-based information. Each control system component needs to be integrated for proper management. The placement of control is shown as the control element in Figure 10.5.

A feedback loop can be from output to the process box giving the historical data information and from the process box to the input to identifying process flaws and hidden factors so that appropriate adjustments can be made. However, there are also the forward feedback loops going in the opposite direction from the input to the processes and from the processes to the output that give valuable information down the line. There is negative and positive feedback referring to information inputs that measure the acceptability of outputs, goals, objectives, and actions taken. Knowing whether the system is on target and producing the desired outcome is the function of all these feedback loops going in both directions.

HOW TO FILL THE GAPS

Filling in the gaps is critical to the ascension of any organization that seeks to reach the pinnacle of success. An example of how to fill the gaps is shown in Figure 3.2, where products/services solutions increase the process yields from 93.3 percent to 99.9 percent identified to fill in the gaps (the level of change needed and how to get there). Appropriate solutions and measurements are applied at each stage for operational excellence and effectiveness. For organization design, the following three methods are suggested for use when aspiring to become world class:

1. Fill gaps through organization design, creating effective organization and operational excellence. Build creative knowledge-based workers and a world-class organization by building self-equity and organizational equity for organizational alignment. Use Malcolm Baldrige's seven criteria of management systems for organization design to build employee self-equity and organization equity.

2. Measure gaps using metrics in a Balance Scorecard Plus format. Use Balanced Scorecard Plus, the four perspectives of Drs. Kaplan and Norton with the addition of information technology and knowledge management for metrics.
3. Mitigate gaps by process improvement through Lean and Six Sigma methodologies. Lean principles and Six Sigma methodologies remove waste and reduce errors in the processes.

CHAPTER

Quality Tools

> *"If we did not make use of quality tools, we would soon find our-selves unable to serve our community well in terms of adding value to the learning experience."*
>
> Dr. Frank K. Toda

Questions are always asked at my lectures or at our site visits: What tools should we use for our organization? What tools exist? Where can I go to find this information? How do I know what to use, which one, and when? What books should I get? It will take another book to describe the entire lot of quality tools. The use of each tool in the quality arena that is best for each organization to enhance the organization's future work plans must be decided by the on-site work managers (Six Sigma Green Belts, Black Belts, Master Black Belts, or Champions).

There are many tools available in the quality arena and many books are written about the subject—too many to list here. However, I will attempt to give you some flavor of the more popular tools in vogue. As you begin to answer your own questions, these may be useful in determining appropriate use of the quality tools for your organization's need. Some quality tools that you might use are found in books in the Bibliography and the Web sites listed in

Appendix A. A really detailed tool reference is *The Quality Tool Box* by Nancy R. Tague, which gives quality practitioners a choice from a variety of tools for dealing with the wide variety of situations that occur on the road to continuous improvement.

Getting your organization ready before committing to a fully embedded use of quality tools is a critical step in a successful launch to greatness. Whether organizations deploy from the grass roots or middle management or from an enterprise-wide level, it is critical that there be some degree of cultural integration prior to utilizing any of the quality tools.

CREATING THE ORGANIZATIONAL CLIMATE FOR QUALITY

Empowered employees who have a commitment to the organization's mission, vision, values, strategic objectives, and action will feel a sense of ownership of the processes and continuous and never-ending quality initiatives and improvements.

Business, operational, and process subunits have the responsibility to tie closely with the goals, strategies, and actions of the parent company corporate offices. In assisting in this endeavor, the organization's business unit operations responsibilities ultimately include being good stewards for the parent corporation. To promote seamlessness, each unit must have a seat at the table to determine what critical and strategic decisions they need to engender to move the organization upward toward achieving a customer-focused environment, where customer satisfaction, delight, and success would be available through the use of quality tools.

Then, with a clear vision to become a world-class organization, the organization should go through transformational change. The concept of this transformation was described in Chapter 4.

Relationship building through management by walking around, one-on-one perception checks, meetings to create awareness for a world-class culture, and a sense of what a quality journey entailed would be a series of steps toward becoming world class.

ARTICULATING THE QUALITY VISION IN A STRATEGIC PLAN

To articulate the quality vision, organizations must implement the strategic plan with a persistent and consistent message in conducting world-class operatives. In my organization I personally got involved in training our original staff members regarding implementing many initiatives, such as transformational leadership, relationship leadership, and employees as leaders looking at doing the "right things" in place of doing "things right." I invited external communities to visit our operations. By inviting the external communities locally, nationally, and internationally to see why we do, what we do, and how we do it, our business units had to look at what is involved in running a fact-based, data-driven, data-informed, and knowledge-based operation, and then explain it to the other entities. I provided a structured methodology of this process to achieve a world-class destiny, a road map, on our Web site: http://www.fpm.iastate.edu/worldclass/.

CREATING THE KEY DRIVERS TO PUSH THE VISION INTO OPERATIONAL EXCELLENCE

The key drivers will be the core values described in a parent corporation's strategic plan. These values are important to business units in the organization to anchor onto for the policy deployment. Some of these could follow the following rendition:

- Responsive (a sense of urgency): Responsiveness to our clients and stakeholders
- Team player (agility and cooperation): Coordination among university entities working in concert with each other
- Value-added (process management oriented): Efficient, accountable, and measurable resource allocation
- Commitment (good stewardship): Involved with our constituents' community

- Professional (provide first-class service): Expand partnerships with other institutions, including governmental entities and the private sector
- Objective (focused on continuous quality improvement): Accountability and rigorous assessment of progress

QUALITY TOOLS

Before implementing any of the quality tools, enterprises should consider developing a continuous quality improvement roadmap for each business unit to help expedite deployment. In our case, we now have in place approximately 108 process maps charted, giving us a unique insight into where we are in the continuum of the quality initiatives and what we need to do to fill in the gaps.

Having common quality tools and processes well mapped from the as-is condition, ratcheting up to the should-be condition and ultimately to the could-be condition, enables the leadership to move our organization toward more conducive common cultural and behavioral patterns throughout the entire management system. We provide common performance management practices to accelerate the creation of a high-performing organization as follows:

- In viewing an issue or a problem, first accept or recognize that conditions are happening that require attention.
- By defining your issues or problems succinctly, you give them boundaries within which to obtain desired outcomes. This sometimes is known in the project management industry as scope of work, showing the magnitude and type.
- Measuring progress for solution implementation verifies whether the remedy has made significant improvements or changes.
- Improve the processes.
- Analyze the situation and find remedies to take corrective action or introduce new steps to modify or enhance processes to solve the issue or problem at hand.

- Control the events occurring so that unbiased repeatable actions will take place that work to make your goods, products, and services better, cheaper, and faster.
- Integrate the successes with the entire operation or organization.

Not all quality tools are applicable for any one organization to improve its processes. You may be using different sets as you determine your needs and where you are in the continuum in the process improvement journey. However, any organization will benefit from using the following:

- Malcolm Baldrige National Quality Award seven criteria of management systems (leadership, strategic planning, customer and market focus, information and analysis, creative human resource focus, process management, and business results) to build staff self-equity and organizational equity. See *Campus Facilities News*, March 2004 Issue, "Comprehensive Facilities Management." Copies of the article can be obtained from the editor kathleen@therobincompany.com or the author.
- Balanced Scorecard Plus perspectives for metrics and performance measures using Kaplan and Norton's four criteria of financial, customer focus, internal processes, innovation, and growth with two additional criteria—information technology and knowledge management to develop critical success factors through focused key performance indicators. See "Metrics," *Campus Facilities News*, January 2005. Copies of the article can be obtained from the editor kathleen@therobincompany.com or the author
- Integrated Lean and Six Sigma principles and methodologies for optimal benefit of the university by reducing waste, removing non-value-added processes, mistake- and error-proofing, and establishing a near-perfection modus operandi toward a zero variance. See *Campus Facilities News*,

September/October issues. Also see *Buildings Magazine*, "Measuring What Matters: Doing Things Right with Six Sigma" in the August 2004 issue, and "Who's Who in the Building Market 2004" (http://www.buildings.com/articles/detail.aspx? contentID=2014).

Quality Tool Box

1. The American Society for Quality (http://www.asq.org/ learn-about-quality/quality-tools.html) provides many quality tools for use in solving problems, and these are neatly arranged in eight categories:

2. Cause analysis tools—fishbone (Ishikawa) diagram, Pareto chart, and scatter diagrams. These tools could be the first step an organization uses for its process improvements by identifying the cause of the problem or situation and then applying other processes and tools to solve the problem.

3. Evaluation and decision-making tools—decision matrix and multivoting tools to narrow a group of choices to arrive at the best one. This process allows you to make informed decisions and helps you choose the best options for a combination of a number of ideas and solutions with a simple objective rating system that determines the success of your project.

4. Process analysis tools—flowchart, failure mode, effect and analysis, mistake-proofing, sometimes known as poke-a-yoke (zero defects). These tools help to identify and eliminate unnecessary process steps in a work flow or an environment to increase productivity and operational excellence through efficiency, reducing time, and cutting costs.

5. Seven basic quality tools—Professor of Engineering Kaoru Ishikawa of Tokyo University is ascribed as the father of "quality circles." QC is known for emphasizing the cause-and-effect diagram, check-list sheet, control charts, Pareto charts, scatter diagram, histogram, and stratification as the seven tools to get to the heart of implementing quality principles.

6. Data collection and analysis tools—uses check sheet, control chart, design of experiment, histogram, scatter diagram, stratification, and survey tools to collect or analyze data.
7. Idea creation tools—organizes many ideas using affinity diagrams, benchmarking, brainstorming, and nominal group technique.
8. Project planning implementation tools—Gantt chart, PDCA.
9. Seven new management and planning tools—(7MP) management and planning tools (see Quality America.com Web site).[1]

The list below includes other information for your quality toolbox.

Activity Network Diagram

This management tool takes a known process, organizes the steps, and determines the critical path and time to accomplish all tasks and subtasks.

Affinity Diagram

The affinity diagram allows you to take what initially seemed a large unrelated grouping of information and organizes it in such a way as to easily recognize new trends or patterns of information.

Bar Chart

Bar charts are used to compare distinct noncontiguous items. The data points are drawn as proportionally side-by-side or stacked bars, most useful for comparative information of like issues.

Balanced Scorecard—Strategy and Metric

The history of the Balanced Scorecard began in 1990 when Nolan Norton Institute, the research arm of KPMG, sponsored a year-long, multicompany seminar entitled "Measuring Performance in the Organization of the Future." In 1992 an article in the *Harvard Business Review* by Robert S. Kaplan and David P. Norton entitled "The Balanced Score Card that Drives Performance" preceded their book, *The Balanced Scorecard: Translating Strategy into Action*. The book introduced the Balanced Scorecard as a holistic set of measures for integrated business performance. The scorecard was originally developed to supplement traditional financial measures discovered in the "Corporate Scorecard" that contained performance measures relating to customer delivery, quality, and cycle times of manufacturing processes and effectiveness of new product developments. The book was a best seller, and it became evident that three other performance criteria (customer focus, internal processes, and learning and growth) would become critical measurements for the performance of an organization.

Information technology and knowledge management are added here as the fifth and sixth criteria for performance measurement of an organization aspiring to become a world-class operation. However, the four criteria indicated by Kaplan and Norton are what every organization needs to follow. The Balance Scorecard Plus includes the four criteria of the original Balanced Scorecard plus IT and KM as follows:

1. Financial performance
2. Customer knowledge or focus
3. Internal business processes
4. Learning and growth (innovation and growth)
5. Information technology (IT)
6. Knowledge management (KM)

Baldrige—Organizational Assessment and Review

The Baldrige Organizational Assessment and Review deals specifically with how an enterprise is positioned to respond to domestic and globalization threats and challenges.

Being first to market is not enough! What matters is how an organization listens to the voice of the customers and the voice of the employees, and how it creates customer success and a knowledge-based culture by going beyond customer satisfaction in fulfilling customer needs through evidence-driven, fact-based, data-driven processes. Using Baldrige criteria helps to build self-equity and organizational equity in promoting achievements in operational excellence regarding productivity and efficiency. All these initiatives culminate in bringing about an effective organization through determining critical success factors and developing metrics from key performance indicators that are the key performance drivers.

Benchmarking[2]

Benchmarking is a structured process for comparing your organization's work practices to the best similar practices you can identify in other organizations and then incorporating the best ideas into your own processes.

Brainstorming

Brainstorming is a method for generating a large number of creative ideas in a short period of time. Use brainstorming:

- When a broad range of options is desired.
- When creative, original ideas are desired.
- When participation of the entire group is desired.

Cause-and-Effect Diagram

The cause-and-effect diagram (also called Ishikawa or fishbone chart) identifies many possible causes for an effect or problem and sorts ideas into useful categories.

Check Sheet

A check sheet is a generic tool that can be adapted for a wide variety of purposes; the check sheet is a structured, prepared form for collecting and analyzing data.

Change Management (Behavior Psychology)[3]

Fred Nikols in his "Change Management 101: A Primer" describes this topic thoroughly. He says there are four basic definitions in thinking about change management:

- The task of managing change
- An area of professional practice
- A body of knowledge
- A control mechanism
- An understanding of the cultural and spiritual domain

I added the fifth definition that must be part of the change management definition. The process is to understand which culture you are dealing with and what spiritual motivation drives that culture in the individual or the organization.

Control Chart

A control chart is a graph used to study how a process changes over time. Comparing current data to historical control limits leads to conclusions about whether the process variation is consistent (in control) or is unpredictable (out of control, affected by special causes of variation).

Continuous Quality Improvements[4]

This is a management philosophy which contends that most things can be improved. This philosophy does *not* subscribe to the theory that "If it ain't broke, don't fix it." It focuses on process rather than the individual; it recognizes both internal and external customers; and it promotes the need for objective data to analyze and improve processes.

Cultural Transformation Tools[5]

Cultural transformation tools are the invention of Richard Barrett and Associates. Richard Barrett in his book *Building a Values-Driven*

Organization: A Whole System Approach to Cultural Transformation,[6] Elsevier-Sabre Foundations, 2006, uses seven levels of organizational consciousness to make a personal and a corporate cultural assessment by mapping organizational values and personal values derived from an adaptation and extension of Maslow's hierarchy of human needs, namely: physiological, safety, love/belonging, self-esteem, and self actualization.

Datasheet

Data are used to organize and manage and track data as well as to calculate relationships among data. Data entries are done in a table format of rows and columns or single cards.

Deming Cycle

The Deming cycle also known as PDCA or PDSA cycle is a continuous improvement cycle that looks at four steps. Walter A. Shewhart originally developed the PDCA cycle. He was a Bell Laboratories scientist who was Deming's friend, mentor, and the developer, in the late 1920s, of statistical process control; sometimes this is referred to as the "Shewhart Cycle." There are also several recent variations on this concept (see *The Man Who Discovered Quality* by A. Gabor, Penguin Books, 1990).

Design of Experiment

Design of experiment became one of the most popular statistical techniques used in the 1990s. Many of the current statistical approaches to designed experiments originated from the work of R. A. Fisher in the early part of the 20th century. Its popularity regained when a Japanese engineer, Genichi Taguchi, focused on the practical use versus the mathematical perfection of the technique.

EFQM Excellence Model

The EFQM Excellence Model[7] introduced at the beginning of 1992 is equivalent to the Baldrige criteria for the European entities.

The European Foundation for Quality Management (EFQM) is a not-for-profit organization established in 1989 by various chief executive officers of 14 prominent European companies, such as AB Electrolux, British Telecom, Dassault Aviation, Fiat, KLM, Nestle, Phillips Electronics NV, Renault, and others. The foundation was set up for European enterprises to compete in the global market in improving their competitiveness and effectiveness. This foundation launched the European Quality Award in 1991.

Failure Evaluation Mode Analysis (FEMA)

Begun in the 1940s by the U.S. military, FEMA was further developed by the aerospace and automotive industries. It is a step-by-step approach for identifying all possible failures in a design, a manufacturing or an assembly process, or a product or service.

Force Field Analysis

The American social psychologist Kurt Levin is credited with having developed force field analysis using force field diagrams.

Fishbone Diagram

See Ishikawa Diagram and Cause and Effect description below, also called cause-and-effect diagram.

Histogram

The most commonly used graph for showing frequency distributions, or how often each different value in a set of data occurs. It looks very much like a bar chart, but there are important differences.

Interrelationship Digraph

The interrelationship digraph can take ideas from the affinity diagram, or any other source, and show how they relate to one another.

Often used as a tool to determine the underlying causes of situations; an interrelationship digraph can easily allow you to see which causes are fundamental to the solution.

Ishakawa Diagram

This is also known as the cause and effect diagram or root cause analysis. Root cause analysis is a class of problem-solving methods aimed at identifying the root causes of problems or events.

ISO 9000

These are process improvement controls (verification and clarification). In 1946 delegates from 25 countries met in London and decided to create a new international organization. The object would be "to facilitate the international coordination and unification of industrial standards." The new organization, The International Standards Organization, officially began operations in February 1947 in Geneva, Switzerland.[8]

There are two standards developed by ISO that are widely known: ISO 9000 and ISO 14000. ISO 9000 is primarily concerned with quality management. Organizations fulfill their needs through viewing:

1. Customer quality requirements
2. Applicable regulatory requirements
3. Enhanced customer satisfaction
4. Continual improvement of performance

Lean—Reduction in Waste

Taiichi Ohno and Dr. Shigeo Shingo are the co-inventors of Lean, "The Toyota Production System," covering how to improve the overall process of production in manufacturing, popularized in America by two top industrial analysts, James Womack and Daniel Jones, after they wrote their landmark book *The Machine That*

Changed the World. Womack and Jones explained that companies can dramatically improve their performance using Lean production techniques. Lean thinking concepts and production pioneered by Toyota look at production (operations) differently from processes of manufacturing. Making this separation allowed Taiichi Ohno and Dr. Shingo to recognize that the biggest gains for improvement come from shortening the manufacturing time line and eliminating the non-value-added wastes

Dr. Shingo taught Toyota and other Japanese companies the art of identifying and solving problems on his scientific thinking mechanism, which fundamentally taught how to identify and solve problems. Virtually everyone at Toyota is taught how to solve problems around his or her work area and to be involved every day in improvement activities. Dr. Shingo was most known in the West for his SMED (single-minute exchange of dies) and poka-yoke (mistake-proofing) systems.

In his book, *Kaizen and the Art of Creative Thinking*, Dr. Shingo explains the ethos of Toyota's production system, with examples of how other companies benefited and struggled with these principles. In the book, Dr. Shingo presents six unique models, the sum of which he calls the scientific thinking mechanism. It embodies techniques and philosophies advocated by others, such as the aforementioned experimental scientific thinking, creative thinking, and brainstorming methods. Although each of these methods captured a certain aspect, none of them were comprehensive. Thus, he combined the strengths of these various methods and created this scientific thinking mechanism. Fredrick Taylor, Immanuel Kant, and W. E. Deming—well known to all college business students—developed some of these methods. The following is the genesis guide to the foundations of the Toyota Production System:

Principles of Analytical Thinking

- Capturing problems
- Idea generation for improvement

- The evolution of improvement
- From ideas to reality
- Promoting improvement ideas
- Quick and easy kaizen

Management and Planning Tools

Using 7MP Tools in planning avoids the guesswork and the rework of any project. One no longer needs to rely on hit and miss techniques. Using the Management and Planning 7MP Tools can take a seemingly complex, abstract idea and narrow it down to an understandable, orderly plan of action—considering the specific tasks to undertake, the time to complete them, and the order in which to complete them. Net effect: cycle time reduction, reduced waste, better service.

Matrix Diagram

The matrix diagram is used to rate the correlation between groups of ideas to achieve agreement on the most critical for decision making.

Nominal Group Technique

Nominal group technique is a structured method for group brain-storming that encourages contributions from everyone on the team.

Pareto: 80/20 Rule[9]

The Italian economist Vilfredo Pareto (1848–1923) introduced Pareto's law of income distribution. He observed that 80 percent of income in Italy went to 20 percent of the population. It has become a common rule of thumb in business to say that 80 percent of your sales come from 20 percent of your clients. Or, in other situations like an organization, that 80 percent of the problems are caused by 20 percent of your workforce. Another measure is that 20 percent of the employees in your organization perform more of the bulk of the tasks than 80 percent of the rest of the cohorts. Joseph M Juran, noted quality guru, introduced the Pareto principle, the 80-20 rule. He said that the law of the vital few and the principle of factor sparsity state that for many events, 80 percent of the effects come from 20 percent of the causes.

Process Management

Process management is the ensemble of activities of planning and monitoring the performance of a process, especially in the sense of business process, often confused with reengineering. Process management is the application of knowledge, skills, tools, techniques, and systems to define, visualize, measure, control, report, and improve processes with the goal to meet customer requirements profitably. It is different from project management, which is concerned with managing a group of interdependent projects.

Project Management

On time, on budget, and on scope—project management is the discipline of organizing and managing resources (e.g., people) in such a way that the project is completed within defined scope, quality, time, and cost constraints. A project is a carefully defined set of activities that use resources (money, people, materials, energy, space, provisions, communication, etc.) to meet the predefined objectives.[10]

Quality Circles

The term *quality circles* was coined in Japan in 1961. The Union of Japanese Scientists and Engineers (UJSE) sponsored the research, which combined the theories of behavior science with quality control concepts and techniques under the leadership of Dr. Kaoru Ishikawa, an engineering professor at Tokyo University.[11]

Tree Diagram

Once the important issues are apparent, increasing levels of detail use the Tree Diagram to stratify ideas. The Tree Diagram helps take broad goals or ideas and narrow them into specific assignments, tasks, or options.

Quality Function Deployment

Yoji Akao originally developed QFD in 1966 when the author combined his work in quality assurance and quality control points with function deployment used in value engineering.

Scatter Diagram

The scatter diagram graph pairs numerical data with one variable on each axis, to look for a relationship between them. If the variables are correlated, the points will fall along a line or curve.

Shingo

Deming Award for Excellence winner Shigeo Shingo (1909-1990), born in Saga City, Japan, was a Japanese industrial engineer who distinguished himself as one of the world's leading experts on manufacturing practices and the Toyota Production System. Shingo is known far more in the West than in Japan as a result of his meeting Norman Bodek, an American entrepreneur and founder of Productivity Inc. in the USA. In 1981 Bodek had traveled to Japan to learn about the Toyota Production System and came across books by Shingo, who as an external consultant had been teaching industrial engineering courses in Toyota since 1955. Shingo had written his *Study of the Toyota Production System* in Japanese and had it translated, very poorly, into English in 1980. Norman Bodek took as many copies of this book as he could to the USA and arranged to translate Shingo's other books into English, eventually having his original study retranslated. Bodek also brought Shingo to lecture in the USA and developed one of the first Western Lean manufacturing consultancy practices with Shingo's support.

The myth prevails that Shingo invented the Toyota Production System. However, he documented the system and added two terms to the Japanese and English languages: Poka-yoke ("mistake-proofing," *not* "foolproofing," which Shingo rejected as a term) and single-minute exchange of dies (SMED). In 1988, Utah State University recognized Dr. Shingo for his lifetime accomplishments and created the Shingo Prize that recognizes world-class, Lean organizations.

Shingo is the author of numerous books including: *A Study of the Toyota Production System; Revolution in Manufacturing: The SMED System; Zero Quality Control: Source Inspection and the Poka-yoke System; The Sayings of Shigeo Shingo; Key Strategies for Plant Improvement; Non-Stock Production: The Shingo System for Continuous Improvement;* and *The Shingo Production Management System: Improving Process Functions.*

Six Sigma

Six Sigma is a registered trademark of the Motorola Corporation. It is a business process that allows companies to drastically improve their bottom line by designing and tracking everyday business activities in ways that minimize waste (*muda*) and resources while increasing customer satisfaction. Six Sigma is a collection of statistical tools that can be applied to solve tough business and technical problems to reduce variation. Detection of flaws 3.4 defects parts per million is a Six Sigma goal. The detailed process mapping, FMEA (failure mode and effects analysis), MSE (measurement system evaluation), NEM (numerical evaluation of metrics), and DOE (design of experiments) thoroughly evaluate issues using the appropriate tools from the toolkit. The process use is DMAIC (define, measure, analyze, improve, control), IMAIC (identify, measure, analyze, improve, control), and MAIC (measure, analyze, improve, control).

Sigma is also a measure of variability that indicates how much of the data—such as product and service quality, just-in-time (JIT) delivery, or other critical measures of customer satisfaction—fall within the customer's expectations and satisfaction. The narrower the bandwidth of the sigma bell curve and the higher the value of "process sigma," the fewer defects or waste per million parts of a manufacturing or transactional process.

Statistical Process Control

This is an effective method of monitoring a process through the use of control charts, with its emphasis on early detection and prevention of problems.

Survey

Data collected from targeted groups of people about their opinions, behavior, or knowledge.

Stratification

A technique that separates data gathered from a variety of sources so that patterns can be seen.

Theory of Constraints

In 1984 manufacturing guru, Eliyahu M. Goldratt, popularized the Theory of Constraints (constraints, alignment, and policy alignment). It is based on the application of scientific principles and logic reasoning to guide human-based organizations.

TRIZ

This is the acronym for the Theory of Inventive Problem Solving in Russian.[12] The acronym in English is TIPS.

Total Quality Management

This is a management philosophy, originated in the 1950s, that seeks to integrate all organizational functions (marketing, finance, design, engineering, production, customer service, etc.) to focus on meeting customer needs and organizational objectives. The process requires quality in all aspects of the company's operations, with processes being done right the first time and defects and waste eradicated from operations.[13]

Dr. W. Edwards Deming popularized total quality management and is credited for improving production in the United States during World War II and after that in Japan. Deming, who is considered by many to be the father of modern quality control, made the plan-do-check-act (PDCA) cycle for continuous improvement popular; however, he always referred to it as the "Shewhart cycle."

NOTES

1. http://www.qualityamerica.com/QAProducts/7mp-pciv.htm.
2. http://www.asq.org/learn-about-quality/benchmarking/overview/tutorial.html.
3. http://home.att.net/~nickols/change.htm.
4. http://www.fpm.iastate.edu/worldclass/cqi.asp.
5. http://www.google.com/search?hl=en&q=CTT—Cultural+Transformation+Tools&btnG=Google+Search.
6. Richard Barrett, *Building a Values-Driven Organization: A Whole System Approach to Cultural Transformation*, Elsevier-Sabre Foundations, 2006.
7. http://www.efqm.org/Default.aspx?tabid=35.
8. http://www.iso.org/iso/about/discover-iso_meet-iso/discover-iso_isos-origins.htm.
9. http://cepa.newschool.edu/het/profiles/pareto.htm.
10. http://en.wikipedia.org/wiki/Process_management#_note-0#_note-0 and http://en.wikipedia.org/wiki/Project_management.
11. http://www.ie.boun.edu.tr/course_pages/ie483/QC.html.
12. http://www.triz-journal.com/whatistriz_orig.htm.
13. http://www.isixsigma.com/library/content/c031008a.asp.

Trends Facing a World-Class Journey

> *"Only those who risk going too far, can possibly find out how far they can go."*
>
> T. S. Eliot

CUSTOMER SUCCESS SIGNIFICANCE

Customer Success as an idea for me personally has withstood the test of time. I have been presenting, teaching, coaching, and mentoring to my respected colleagues and audiences across the globe on creating a world-class operation. For many years the fact has become clearer to me each day that no organization will be able to reach the pinnacle of success and maintain its stature without the philosophy of customer success to gain customer significance.

Customer Success is the way of the future to assure bringing any organization to a world-class operative with a values-based organizational philosophy. As I look back, the concept of customer success was ingrained in me in very early childhood. I learned it from the many vendors in the simple bazaars in India, located on the south slopes of the great Himalayan mountain range along the borders of Nepal, Sikkim, West Bengal, and Bhutan. In the land of the thunderclouds where those small merchants made sure their customers were significant and successful, they made a mark in my life. They adopted a way of marketing that assured customer success relationships beyond satisfaction and beyond customer delight. Every week they religiously brought their fruits, vegetables, and animal merchandise to market from their small farms and gardens.

Every Wednesday and Saturday my mother took me to the bazaars shopping for our weekly family food. We would invariably end up shopping with our usual set of vendors before venturing forth to other vendors. At these other vendors, mother handed cash for goods. However, at the regular merchants, the ones we always visited first, she did not give as much cash for the goods and products that she purchased. It always puzzled me and I never quite understood then why mom made a beeline to the vendors she had a relationship with first, and then later to those who had different goods and products, not available with her regulars. Until one day I heard mom telling one of the regular merchants that she did not have enough money to pay for the food and products that we needed. However, she would be able to make it up to them the following week. She explained that when we next returned, she would have more cash. It dawned on me; mom never fully had the means to pay for what we needed. These shopping encounters were repeated biweekly, and mom never seemed to have enough budgeted cash to reimburse the merchant on the day of the purchase.

I now understand completely the principle of customer success and personal relationships.

The merchants created the environment for a steady loyal customer for their business. Those vendors with whom mom had a unique relationship were successful because they knew they would sell their goods and products every week without fail.

No one knows how deep the impacts of customer success relationships go. They will be the purview of many organizations as they begin to inculcate these precepts into their future workers.

There is a loss to the customer if an organization focuses on only satisfying the customer. In the long run you may still lose their goodwill. Your organization may have short-term gains but at what cost? However, focusing on customer success and customer well-being in every aspect, especially financially, will reap your organization bountiful benefits for the near term, short term, and long term. Developing an organization that knows customer focus is to give your customer three options—satisfaction, delight, and success. But making customer success a repeatable and continuous process is the primary challenge in the future for any organization.

WARP TO HYPERSPEED AGE

This age of undue hurry and confusion at warp speed, hyperspeed, hyperconnectedness, and hypertransparency is causing extraordinary upheaval on an evolutionary scale with unprecedented developments around the globe of gargantuan proportions, hitherto unimaginable. Major paradigm shifts will be changing the face of the earth and making our future business decisions much different from what we know today. Impacts to our environment are happening faster than ever. What are some of the hyperspeed age phenomenon facing tomorrow's world-class organizations with respect to business decisions taking place at warp speed?

POPULATION GROWTH

Disproportionate population growth is expected in a number of countries, and the aging population, as they retire, is reducing the per capita "knowledge workers" for tomorrow's workforce. In the stable population period of Julius Caesar's era, it is estimated that the total world population was around 150 million people. By the time Christopher Columbus sailed his ships into the new world, the earth's population had more than doubled to around 500 million. Before the Second World War, the population neared two billion compared to the new world population estimation of six billion, which is expected to grow to around nine billion by the year 2050. Of this tremendous growth, nine countries—India, China, the United States, Pakistan, Nigeria, the Democratic Republic of Congo, Bangladesh, Uganda, and Ethiopia—will account for one-half of the total world population! According to the United Nations Population Division, it is estimated that in the year 2050, the four largest countries in the world will be India, China, Pakistan, and the United States (CSIS Global Aging Initiative) (http://www.csis.org/gai, http://www.un.org/esa/population/unpop.htm, http://www.un.org).

Adding to the exponential population explosion, there is a shifting dynamic of young people. Younger populated nations versus nations with older generations will impinge on the capacity to work and produce, where production will be restricted by the available manpower and each country's ability to support the ever-caring and nurturing needs for the geriatric population as it grows more feeble, but living longer due to better nutrition and medical breakthroughs. Aging populations in some countries will be taxing the young to support the elders and their infrastructure. Migration from farms to cities and more dense urbanization are anticipated to congest existing metropolitan areas, requiring different types of living conditions and situations. Immigration pressures to the developed countries from the developing countries will continue to cause brain drain for those emerging economies in countries wishing to emulate the western thriving sectors. These pressures of immigration will bring knowledge, wealth, and political, language, and cultural diversity, as well as assimilation issues to the nations that the immigrants will be calling their new home.

FOOD SHORTAGES

Scarcity of food is something that is daunting and is not on the immediate radar of many world leaders or multinational corporations. As we keep adding to our population growth, resource management of our arable land will be the focus of the future as the world agriproduction and agrinations will be reaching their limits of diminishing returns. Despite the many advances in chemistry, mathematics, physics, and technology coming to the aid of modern farming, food shortages are anticipated.

Arable land and production limits per acre will be stretched beyond the yield capacity. Fields are being optimized beyond production capacity even with the best of the best husbanding of agricultural resources. It appears under the current belief paradigm, no amount of increase in science and technology can coax production from the limited land and already tired soil. As not having fair, manageable resources confront nations, opportunities and threats will come to the fray. Poor past practices in land management—pointed out in Allan Savory's *Holistic Management: A New Framework for Decision Making*, Island Press, 1999, regarding overuse of fertilizers and mismanagement of land use—are causing land degradation, soil erosion, and desertification of agricultural areas on a massive scale. Mismanagement ranges from the deep, simple, ever-expanding open spaces of the jungles of the Amazon to the overcrowded, overpopulated Yangtze River basin. Global warming changes in weather patterns around the globe are bad news for those relying on steady growth patterns. How can we feed all the hungry of the world? What are world-class organizations going to do to stem the tide of hunger and bring humanity to at least fulfilling Abraham Maslow's levels of physical, emotional, mental, and spiritual needs? We are already experiencing water shortages, which preclude expansion of current food production in the world.

WATER SCARCITY

Some say water scarcity may cause us to rely on our neighboring friends in Canada for potable water. A supposed abundance of fresh water is available from the far north for our farm production and human consumption. Such natural wealth for those countries endowed with water will position them well in the foreseeable future to be able to share. They will decide how to dispense this life-giving commodity to those on the receiving end. As we in the western world flush our toilets, we would be guilty each time of using up a week's supply of drinkable water that could save lives in the arid lands and drought-ridden areas of the rest of the world.

Some of this scarcity is attributed to global warming in those parts of the countries where once water was an unending reservoir for cheap hydroelectric energy for their economies. The island of Puerto Rico is said to be experiencing a shortfall of rain, causing them to power down their hydroelectric production. Who is going to apportion this life-giving natural resource to quench the never-ending thirsts around the world? Water shortage for a thirsty world with water scarcity caused by growth of population in the world of fast-paced, economic, and industrialization development is taking place with increasing speed. Food production needs are placing an increasing stress on the finite natural resources of both land and water.

It is said that by the year 2050 more than 54 countries—home to almost four billion people, nearly half the population on the planet—will be facing very serious difficulties in meeting their water demands. The hopes and aspirations for economic development seem to be getting further and further away from the grasp of many aspiring nations. How could they ever hope to catch up with the developing countries? Such a pressure keg situation caused by such disparity and inequality could pose dire consequences for all those individuals and organizations. In the eye of these brewing storms, the existing and continuing conflicting wants, needs, and requirements will dominate the next century.

ENERGY DEMANDS

With the conflicting issues of the price of oil rising in the world and the increase in energy consumption by nations and organizations, there is a conflict between what is good for the planet and what is needed for growth. The younger generations—after the baby boomers and the X and the Y generations—will be the new leaders in the world. They are genuinely concerned and focused on sustainability, doing what is necessary to save the planet earth.

> *"We do not inherit the earth from our ancestors; we borrow it from our children."*
>
> Native American proverb

The global demand for energy is pushing some countries like China and others to continue to use the fossil fuel coal for their power and electric consumption, adding significantly to pollution. The increase in reliance on hydrocarbon coal, oil, and gas by significant numbers of nations in the world for their energy will cause emissions to further exacerbate the already growing concerns of the impact of global warming. As other developing nations in Asia continue to drive the demand for hydrocarbons, those countries' aggregate increase of alternative energy sources will be overshadowed by the exponential consumption of coal, oil, and natural gas. In the foreseeable future, what does this mean for those world-class organizations in the midst of this energy demand? How can we change the mindset of the coming generation to conserve and use less energy? Will there be less apprehensiveness for nuclear fuel to generate electricity if we could dispose of the spent fuel? How much energy will we need as computation power continues to increase voraciously in seemingly endless quantities?

COMPUTATION

Technological advances have exponentially exploded the bit of information that can be manipulated. During the period from 1939 to 1942, Professor Atanasoff with the help of graduate student, Clifford Berry, assembled and demonstrated the first electronic digital computer named the Atanasoff-Berry Computer (ABC). They used the binary system of arithmetic (1s and 0s), separate memory, computing processors, regenerative memory, electronic amplifiers using the 1s and 0s as on-off switches, parallel processing, circuits for logical addition and subtraction, clocked control of electronic operations, and modular design construction. Although it took hours to compute simple mathematics, it was the first electronic digital computer and the first parallel electronic digital computer.

When my brother-in-law was working for Jet Propulsion Laboratory in Sacramento, California, it took a whole room-sized computer to crunch all night the bits of information to produce results the next morning. Today my Smart phone probably computes as much information as those colossal machines and it does so in a few seconds. My two-pound portable Dell 430 Latitude laptop absorbs the hundreds of e-mails I get every day and stores them for retrieval at a moment's notice. The communication devices we see on the horizon are doing marvelous things never done before. The media players that occupy children and adults alike and the onboard navigation systems we installed in the university's KingAir turbo jet are just a few examples of how technology has already made computational power and networking information so powerful that organizations can keep their knowledge management current and available at their fingertips.

We leveraged technology at our organization to change mindset and behavior patterns to see business improvements in a different light. At FP&M we "webbified" our operations with almost 2635 websites, and we computerized facilities management systems. How much computation power will be there in the future? What kinds of data warehousing facilities will be present? How much energy will we need? These are questions that a brave new world order is anticipating for our world-class organizations.

TECHNOLOGICAL GROWTH

Technological growth becomes mind-boggling as computing power grows the demand for more energy, resources, skills, and knowledge. We have moved from bytes only a few years ago to megabytes, gigabytes, terabytes to teraflops and now from teraflops to megaflops to petaflops in computing speed and power. It is said that in June 2005, IBM's two eServers Blue Gene Solution computers achieved computational capacities of 280 teraflops (280 trillion calculations per second) and 114 teraflops, respectively, making them the most powerful supercomputers in the world (http://www. tap500.org). It is no longer the case that the advance of robotics with artificial intelligence is just a novel playground. With computing capacity achieving almost human brain computational proportions, it is anticipated that an almost human-like machine is possible in the near future. Or is the age of machines taking over human beings here already? How will world-class organizations deal with these new machine workers and how will they deal with those humans left out of the food chain?

With technological issues come privacy issues. Our leaders definitely will be challenged by new ethical complexities and public and private policy issues when presented with the unprecedented levels of control over crops, livestock, human life, and bountiful data. Who will be permitted to view all this data? How can we data mine all this information for the good of all concerned without impinging on privacy issues? Who will be the repository of this data and what data?

Former Federal Reserve Chairman Alan Greenspan coined the term *weightless economy*—an economy in which knowledge and technical capacity assume ever more significant positions relative to the "material" world. Author Tom Friedman has said the world is flat; hence, he bets that distances will no longer bind students and entrepreneurs of the developing world as technology continues to reach these workers instantly in the far corners of the globe. They will compete directly with the developed world. How are world-class organizations positioning their knowledge workers to compete in this environment?

Already companies are working on the "how" of their value-based operational principles—the think, behave, and lead parts of their organizations as compared to "what" they produce. In order to innovate and differentiate from its competitors, an organization must focus more on "how" it does things. This new emphasis can serve to distinguish an organization from the already crowded market of "what" companies do to fend off reverse engineering in producing goods, products, and services, better, cheaper, and faster than the originator. Information is perishable and must be constantly renewed with technological growth. In a knowledge-based economy, continuous retraining and relearning is necessary and relevant to keep up and exceed a competitor's prowess. What does a world-class organization do to keep up with the highly dynamic knowledge-based economy to outwit its competition?

GENETICS AND BIOTECHNOLOGY

The successful mapping of human DNA[1] by Dr. Francis Collins, the director of the International Human Genome Project, and Dr. Craig Venter, president of Celera Genomics, had the world in a buzz with new hopes for new medical treatments. Genome research will bring to attention medicinal needs for an individual's well-being to fit more closely with our individual vital functions, rather than relying on mass-produced pharmaceutical drugs. The new paradigm purports to make adjustments for our individual needs with wonder drugs for a happier, healthier, and perhaps prolonged life through metrics-based health products.

Not far in the future we might expect that our clothing will have the requisite monitoring devices to check our vital stats. "Nanite" micromachines—the vision many years ago of such physicists as Richard Feynman—are now manifesting into microchip saviors through medical science. These tiny, almost invisible to the naked eye, engines of mercy with instrumentation monitoring will be the new guardians of life, constantly and interactively checking our life's bodily vitals for proper functioning. The miracle of microchip technology has certainly come of age to enhance the quality of life.

A human "dashboard" with instrument panels showing vital information in the form of key performance indicators will be available to keep track of critical success factors of a healthy functioning body. Perhaps when you get up in the morning next to your bathroom mirror there will be a visual dashboard showing your vital statistics—a report of your body's vital signs taken throughout the night. Or, perhaps your good night's sleep is a consequence of a highly sophisticated automonitoring of your vital signs by your personal dashboard instrument panel—the guardian monitors help you to adjust and correct all minor defects while you sleep peacefully. Such instrumental panels could be mounted at any place of convenience or be available to you on a screen strapped onto a wristwatch device like Dick Tracy's classic comic strip fantasy radio and TV watch.

The fact that such metrics can easily be deployed for our personal use is mind-boggling. Appropriate dispensing of medicine or food prescribed to meet our individual needs is not an impossible proposition anymore. The technology for the management of such processes is here without need for the intervention of human hands. The smart refrigerator will recognize individual profiles and will order appropriate food as items are used. Coffee is ready for you in the morning; food is cooked as a balanced diet prepared just right for you. The smart kitchen countertop, providing recipes with proper calories and appropriate ingredient measurements for your favorite meals, is not far-fetched. Evidence is mounting as we speak of such amazing things as intelligent shopping carts, which calculate the quantity and determine the price of items as you shop around, which give you the final total of your purchases.

The Star Trek electro/chemical/mechanical humanoid with instrumentation, the "Borg," is not such a far-fetched idea either. Some of these artifacts were being displayed in the halls of the Republican and Democratic conventions. The art of instant pictorial transmission reporting to the Internet is here. "Borg" technology, once the domain of the trekkies, will begin to invade all our lifestyles. This points to our need for profound knowledge and understanding of the processes which are going to take place in the future. The new customer focus thinking and catering to the niche market is already evident with companies now developing products and services driven by their customers' preferences and needs though metrics. This latest state of mind caters to a more demanding sophisticated customer of the new age. A good example is Domino Pizza's profiling metrics of its customers' choices and delivering the goods to the individual clients. The old paradigm, when mass production was the norm and satisfied a less demanding customer base, was a more universal solution in a nonexistent competitive market structure.

NANOTECHNOLOGY

At one of his presentations, Erick Peterson, senior vice president at the Center for Strategies and International Studies in Washington, D.C., divulged that micro-electromechanical machines (MEMs), smaller than dust mites and formed out of microscopic gears, chains, and computer chips, were already being deployed in medicine, agriculture, supply chain management, materials science, manufacturing, and warfare.

Nanotechnology—the manipulations of individual atoms and molecules to make novel materials, devices, and systems by constructing matter from its basic building blocks—has been making headlines, capturing our imagination with the promise of creating tiny materials and devices with unprecedented capabilities. It has the potential to radically alter the way we design and fabricate thousands of products now and in the future. Jack Uldrich, president of Minnesota-based Nano Veritas Group and coauthor of *The Next Big Thing Is Really Small*, says, "Everything in our world is made of atoms. And with the ability to manipulate those atoms, the rule of the game for almost every business will be dramatically changed."

Many of the things nanotechnology can potentially enable seem right out of the realm of science fiction from nanobots that will patrol our bloodstream for disease to chameleon-like cars that could assume different colors and shapes. The questions for world-class organizations will be: How will nanotechnology enable the creation of new materials, devices and systems? How will nanotechnology impact the industries of tomorrow? Where are we in this game?

WEAPONS OF MASS DESTRUCTION

There are possibilities of individuals and organizations, not just nations, having their hands on weapons of mass destruction. With the mapping of genomes, we are ready for designer drugs and the scary, foreboding, ominous possibility of superbugs that can annihilate humanity in a wink. What are organizations to do when it is said that what tomorrow's workers will be doing has not even been invented today? Not knowing what they will be working on, how do they get ready for such dynamic shifts?

SENSE OF URGENCY

Why is there such an urgency to create a world-class operation in every arena? To seek answers to these questions, we must look at some world trends that are out there for us to fathom and determine the foggy, uncertain future.

One reason for organizations to aspire to become world class is the impact now being felt by globalization across the brave new world of the 21st century, where everything is moving exponentially at warp speed. To understand the nuances of all that is taking place and to absorb the impacts, we need to put in place an organization that is moving toward near perfection, moving toward a world-class operation.

There will be increasing numbers of people moving around the world, causing great social, cultural, and economic changes. Getting a new generation of workers equipped to deal with these changes is not easy. Dealing with the challenges of the current reality is operating at the survival level. To get past this survival mode, we must look to the future and plan for what can be, should be, and could be levels of excellence.

Survival mode performance is average performance; it is just doing enough, but not enough to compete in the global market—being at the leading edge of things and sustaining that position, not enough to become world class. The leading-edge approach to become world class is to practice and to achieve the highest performance level for any organization relentlessly, without compromise. It should be the ambition of any organization to achieve that ultimate goal of reaching a world-class stature, becoming an outstanding organization, the best of the best.

The World Bank predicts that the population will grow from five to seven billion between now and 2030 (roughly 22 years from now), and there will be a staggering 40% increase with many more mouths to feed in countries where the daily wage is now less than $2, and even today they are unable to feed themselves. In the 1980s, 7.9 million people legally entered the United States, 7.3 million people legally entered the rest of the industrial world, and 100 million people moved from poor countries in the third world, like some from the Philippines to Singapore and other parts of the world.

Another five or six million people have illegally migrated into the industrial world, and in the United States alone, there is a yearly influx of a million illegal aliens. Current estimates from news polls indicate approximately 12 to 20 million illegal aliens are already impacting the U.S. economy and effecting societal changes. The world has never seen this kind of migration from poor countries to rich countries. At the same time the trends in the demographics regarding who is coming down the pipeline in America are alarming, as shown by the figures from the U.S. Department of Commerce:

The Bureau of the U.S. Department of Commerce census taken in 2005 indicates there is another factor that organizations should note: the U.S. workforce of the future will be changing drastically. The U.S. workforce will be smaller because of the elderly population increase of 80% by the year 2025, while the working age population of adults and children increases by only 15%.

There will be fewer males in the workforce; women will comprise 48% of the workforce by 2015.

The U.S. Department of Labor, International Telework Association and Council, and The Gartner Group indicate that more people are working off-site and more are telecommuting. The number of off-site workers rose from 36 million to 55 million from 1999 to 2004. At the same time, there were changes from 1 million to 1.6 million satellite offices with changes from 5 million teleworkers to 7 million. There was an increase of mobile professionals from 9.2 million to 19 million. The scary part is that in order for an organization to achieve world-class stature it has to draw employees from a pool of applicants who are not ready for tomorrow's jobs.

The U.S. Department of Labor predicts that 75 percent of future jobs will be knowledge-based, yet the current workforce is not ready. The 25- to 34-year-olds have not completed college; 70 percent of the workforce will not be college graduates. Only 21 percent of our current adult population has basic literacy skills, and 75 percent of workers will need retraining. Given these grim statistics, tomorrow's competitive and leading-edge companies and institutions will have to build their cadre of knowledge-based workers from within their organizations and continue to rely on foreign graduates. Given the aftermath of 9/11, more institutions of higher education are experiencing a decline of applications of foreign students as other countries in the world are catching up with U.S. higher education expertise, research, and development from their traditional position of leading edge. The creation of knowledge-based workers is no small task; it will be the survival of future organizations to concentrate on developing future leaders and knowledge workers to think, behave, and lead their organizations to excellence.

KNOWLEDGE-BASED WORKERS

Knowledge-based workers (see Chapter 3) are needed in all organizations for the 21st century. I believe Peter Drucker was the author who coined the term *knowledge workers*, and Ken Blanchard wrote on the idea of an employee of an organization being able to straddle two worlds at the same time—one foot in the existing world with the Deming "profound knowledge" workers and the other foot in the new world of possibilities. Also, someone has said, "It is easier to design tomorrow than to mire yourself in the difficulties of today." In Chapter 3, we discussed the "knowledge-based worker" who has an intimate understanding of his or her areas of interest and endeavor and is uniquely prepared to handle the challenges of tomorrow. The 21st-century organization needs to cultivate knowledge-based workers who are uniquely qualified to understand world-class operatives, to coach and lead people, and to manage, thus providing a home for talented people to harvest the fruits of their labor in a field of opportunities in an organization with unfettered governance and controlled autonomy. Knowledge-based workers are volunteers and not conscripts.

World-class organizations are focused on developing their people through training and development for self-equity that ultimately leads to organization equity. This equity relates to focusing on developing their individual strengths and managing their weaknesses through a learning and teaching environment. This equity leads to creating new products from the mastery of their craft. When employees exit from their comfort zone of certainty into uncertainty, they move to the more satisfying zone of creativity, meaningful work, and fulfillment. Organizations need to ascertain that their intellectual memory is secure, grounded, and reliable. The knowledge worker's asset is the intellectual capital for a world-class organization and will be one of the key performance indicators of success.

SAILING UNCHARTED WATERS

Successful organizations will look at the trends facing their world-class journey and will be implementing many of the features that we have mentioned using quality tools. Today's trend is tomorrow's history. An organization aspiring to become world class has many ways to reach its destination. Earlier we mentioned the expressions "If you do not know where you are going, any road will take you there" or "The journey of a thousand miles begins with a single step." To make any journey, we need a map. Your organization must make your own map and then build the ship uniquely suited for the purpose, objective, and destination of the journey.

There are many ways of mapping the voyage to sail uncharted waters and to reach your safe harbor, your world-class destination. In this book we navigate our path by using the Malcolm Baldrige seven criteria for management systems to develop self-equity and organizational equity. We use Balanced Scorecard Plus to measure what an organization values, and we use Lean and Six Sigma for process improvements. These four systems are already available and being used by many successful enterprises. FP&M at Iowa State University could be the first to use all four of these quality tools in consort, synergistically.

There are many questions that must be answered before your trip is over. Ponder the following questions when creating a road map or making charts (plans, strategic as well as tactical) to guide your organizations:

1. What kind of ship? We use the ship as a metaphor for the kinds of organizations that we will build to take us across uncharted waters on a journey to reach world-class stature.
2. How do we predict the future? By understanding current reality, focusing on the future, and dreaming of an ideal state where we want to dock. State a clear vision, a sense of purpose and the objectives to be reached. To reach our final destination, we must anticipate and understand the challenges and cope with them.
3. What kind of crew? The organization will need to train its employees to steer the ship to its destination. The crew must understand the maps and charts that you and your organization will develop to reach each phase of the journey to world class.

4. How do we know what metrics to use? Each organization must develop its own measures—the right kind of metrics or measurements for the right voyage. If you wish to arrive safely, like the ship of the ancient mariners, you need to accurately measure the distances to cover, the directions to take, the climate to bear, and you need to brace yourselves for the winds and the rising tides of change. Your metrics must measure what matters, selecting the right kinds of key performance indicators to arrive at critical success factors. An airline pilot using dials and meters (the dashboard) constantly monitors and corrects the course of the plane from the beginning of its journey until it lands. On an average flight, an airliner is off course 95% of the time—requiring many minor corrections.

5. How do we check our strategies and tactical plans? Not unlike checking to see if the airplane is on course, we need to pause occasionally to see if we are following the road maps or charts that we developed and if they are working well. We need to check our position from time to time to assure we are not deviating from our course. This requires a well-documented project plan, defining each process. If you do not document your plans, how will you remember what to do long enough to get the job done?

6. What are the promised treasures? What treasures do we bring to the organization at the end of the journey? What is acquired and laden in our ship for the enjoyment of our customers or others? For a corporation it could be financial success on the return of its investments, dividends for the shareholders (the ultimate satisfaction for the stakeholders), success for the customer, personal satisfaction for the individual, and success in finding a home for the many employee talents in the organization where fields of opportunities are waiting to be created. This makes work purposeful, meaningful, and fulfilling for the benefit of all.

7. What kinds of processes and methodologies do we use? As each organization strives to reach near perfection, it must use operatives that minimize waste and reduce variation, and create results that tend toward zero defects. Everything that we do before, during, and after the voyage requires scrutiny, and the processes must be impeccable.

8. What must we do not only to survive, but also to be successful? To meet or exceed customer expectations, we must create "customer satisfaction." To exceed customer satisfaction you must create customer delight (Disney World, Ritz Carlton, and many others know this well) through process management with the modus operandi of one plus more, which means customer success.

9. What do we do to calibrate organizational value? The direction, alignment, and empowerment triad is an important one. The objective is to calibrate each organization's compass to the methods for a smooth, safe, and bountiful arrival to your safe harbor.

NOTE

1. Human Genome Information Project, The White House, June 2000 (www.ornl.gov/hgmis).

Conclusion

The world is getting flatter, and there is no room for error or delays; time is of the essence. Customers expect 24/7 service and individuals and organizations must meet employee and customer wants, needs, and requirements. To meet these demands organizations must continually renew themselves. Delivery of goods, products, or services will go to those organizations able to meet or exceed a customer's expectations. Each company or institution will continue to seek a competitive edge as it positions itself to survive the fierce, aggressive onslaught of local and global competition. "Only those who risk going too far can possibly find out how far they can go."

I think President Eisenhower warned of the might of the military-industrial complex. My wife coined the word *coroporalis* for those multinational corporations that exceed the wealth of some nations that have the power to impact the promise and perils of the challenges of governance of nations on the globe. The new world order will be challenging to many individuals and organizations as they assemble their teams to meet the vision, mission, and values of the organizations that they will be leading in these tumultuous times.

We live in a world where at this time corporations, not countries, manage 13 to 14 of the top 50 economies in the world. Therefore, in an era of proliferation of nongovernmental organizations (NGOs), the challenge for the next generation of leaders is to make sure that the NGOs are not dictatorial and that they do not impact the lives of people such that the government "of the people, by the people, and for the people" is neutralized. The corporations with this power must bear the responsibility for helping to provide for social needs and for addressing the challenges of supplying peoples' wants, needs, and requirements. How can these large corporations with power and wealth more than most nations decide on the health, equity, energy needs, and the feeding of the starving and the quenching of the thirsty? The question for all world-class organizations or those aspiring to be so is to ask how we can inculcate customer success in every walk of life to make customers significant.

You have been exposed to the "why," the "what," and the "how" to take your operatives to the next level of excellence. Achieving excellence should be an aspiration knowing that it is attainable for any organization!

In the beginning of this book I mentioned the "yellow brick road" from the movie the *Wizard of Oz* as a metaphor that any organization could follow for accomplishing a specified goal and reaching the final destination. An organization must have the heart, the brains, and the courage portrayed by the tin man, the scarecrow, and the lion to move forward. Like the heroine, Dorothy, I hope your journey takes you home to fulfillment.

Safe journey, fellow travelers!

Appendix A: Web Resources

ASQ—The American Society for Quality (ASQ) is the world's leading authority on quality, and since 1991 ASQ has administered the United States' premier quality honor—the Malcolm Baldrige National Quality Award, which annually recognizes companies and organizations that have achieved performance excellence. www.asq/who-we-are/index.html.

Nano Electronics Planet, www.nanoelectronicsplanet.com.

Nano Today, www.materialstoday.com/nanotoday.htm.

Quality America, founded in 1983, offers SPC, Six Sigma software, training, and consulting, http://www.qualityamerica.com/.

Small Times, www.smalltimes.com.

Appendix B: Glossary and Abbreviations

AAR: after action review.

ABC: Atanasoff Berry computer.

Academy: online, via internal Web, offering training refresher courses.

APPA: the Association of Physical Plant Administrators. This organization began in 1914 but changed its name to Higher Education Facilities Officers in 1980, while retaining the APPA logo and acronym. In July 2007, the association went through a branding initiative and again kept the APPA logo while changing its tag line to "Leadership in Educational Facilities."

ATEM: Association of Tertiary Education Management.

ASQ: American Society for Quality.

B2B: business to business.

Balanced Scorecard: activities or driver "metrics" for benchmarking and improvement measures initiated by Drs. Kaplan and Norton in 1992.

BM: benchmark, "measuring what matters" with other world-class operatives.

This appendix explains the meaning of abbreviations or acronyms used throughout this book and also attempts to provide definitions or discussions of terms related primarily to the particular contexts in which they are used in this book.

BPR: business process reengineering.

Byte: a unit of measurement, most often consisting of eight bits.

CANEQIAI: continuous and never-ending quality initiative and improvements, pronounced "Can I"; it is greater in scope than continuous quality improvements.

Capability: ability to cope, enabling an organization with the technology, skill, knowledge, and ability to achieve high performance.

Capacity: ability to take in productivity.

CAVE: citizen against virtually everything.

CCS: critical to customer satisfaction.

CEDAC: cause-and-effect diagram and addition of card.

CEO: chief executive officer.

CFOCS: clearly focused on customer success.

COPQ: cost of poor quality.

Could be: this is the ideal state of an operation—world-class operatives with unbiased repeatable goods, products, or services that meet customer expectations)

CQI: continuous quality improvements.

CR: current reality; a state where the organization is currently at the "is" condition from which assessment an organization can move on to the next phase of development through process mapping.

CRM: customer relation management.

CSF: critical success factors cost, quality, delivery, safety, and morale drive Lean manufacturing and production.

CSIS: Center for Strategies and International Studies.

CTCR: critical to customer requirement.

CTCS: critical to customer success.

CTQ: critical to quality.

Culture keepers: these "relations" people normally determine the pace of change in your organization. The old, stable, and predictable ways are the norm. Anything that is future oriented or uncertain they tend to attack with fervor!

Current reality (CR): the as-is condition in an operation.

Current state (CS): existing situation that has not been mapped.

CVA: customer value analysis.

Cycle time (CT): the time it takes the goods, products, or services to move through all the process steps from "cradle to grave," from inception to completion—ready for delivery to the customer, completed on time and within budget with a profit factor.

Dashboard: akin to an automobile or a cockpit dashboard with various meters; red, yellow, green markers; and controls to monitor the well-being of products and services through data and the processes work flow.

Data mining: digging deep into existing and new data to reveal appropriate information for process improvement.

Delivery: In the 21st century, delivery of products, goods, and services are anticipated almost at the speed of thought

Deployment chart: process map configured by entities touch columns.

DFSS: design for Six Sigma.

DMACC: Des Moines Ankeny Community Colleges.

DMAIC: define, measure, analyze, improve, and control.

DOD: Department of Defense.

DPI: difference performance interactions.

DPMO: defects per million opportunities.

DT: downtime, the time lost waiting for the next steps in a process to occur.

EEA: Engineering Excellence Award, given by the American Council of Engineering.

Error-proofing: setting condition in operation to mistake-proof.

Evidence drive: fact-based, data-driven, data-informed, and knowledge-based information.

FAMIS: a computer-aided facility and maintenance information system integrated software package, now owned by Actuate Corporation (e-mail: actuatecorp@actuate.com).

FBL: feedback loop.

FFL: forward feedback loop.

Five S (5s): sort, stabilize, shine, standardize, and sustain.

Flat organization: allowing authority at lower levels without having to go through a pyramid structure like the traditional command control.

Flowchart: graphic representation of the flow of a process.

FPI: facilities performance indicator.

FP&M: Facilities Planning and Management organization at Iowa State University, where the Guiding Coalition (GC) is the senior leadership group.

FS: future state. Future state maps are developed with a desire to experiment and implement novel solutions, what has been described as the "should be" conditions in the Ahoy model for "customer success."

FTE: full-time equivalent.

GC: Guiding Coalition. Term refers to leadership team at the Facilities Planning and Management of Iowa State University.

Gemba: defined as a real place where real action occurs. *Gemba* is a Japanese term meaning "the place where the truth can be found." Others may call it "the value proposition." Masaaki Imai, an international consultant and the chairman of the Kaizen Institute of Japan, describes *gemba* as the "real place" where action occurs; *gemba* is where products are developed and where services are provided by the service center. *Gemba* is now used in management terminology to refer to the "workplace."

Gigabyte: The term is derived from the SI prefix *giga-*; a gigabyte is a unit of information or computer storage composed of either exactly 1 billion bytes (10003, or 109) or (rounded off) about 1.07 billion bytes (10243, or 230).

Good to great: In this book, this expression is the third condition of raising the organization bar to reach outstanding results, arriving at the threshold of an ideal state. A *good* level meets specifications (such as ISO 9000, for example) and reaches the condition of a "moment of truth." A *great* condition is outstanding, exceeding the merely good.

HEFMA: Higher Education Facilities Management Association of South Africa.

HP 3000: a model of Hewlett Packard server computer, originally known as a minicomputer, more powerful than a desktop computer but less than a mainframe. An HP 3000 server was purchased by the FP&M organization in 1982. Hewlett Packard ended full service support for this hardware in 1998 and has been gradually phasing out all support. The operating system program it ran on was also non–Y2K compliant, which led to the decision to seek other means of computing to fulfill FP&M's information technology needs.

HR: human resources.

IDS: ideal state, the "could be" condition described in the Ahoy Model; reaching the pinnacle, competitive, and leading edge.

IMAIC: identify, measure, analyze, improve, and control.

IQC: the Iowa Quality Center established in 1999.

IRPE: Iowa Recognition for Performance Excellence.

ISU: Iowa State University.

Just-in-time (JIT): a scheduling concept that calls for any item needed precisely when needed, not a moment earlier or later.

Kaizen: good change, a philosophy of continual improvement.

Kaizen activities: kaizen strategies to achieve Total Quality Management (TQM), Total Preventative Maintenance (TPM), just in time (JITP), Policy Deployment (PD), and team activities.

Kaizen blitz: an instantaneous team event, quick and easy.

Kaizen concepts: concepts that are understood and practiced in implementing kaizen. These include kaizen and management, process versus results, following the plan-do-check-act (PDCA) model, putting quality first, speaking with data, and treating the next process improvement by listening to the voice of the customer.

Kaizen event: a scheduled event to brainstorm issues or problems.

Kanban: an information system in the form of a card that signals the "pull" required to produce the product or services in the needed quantities.

Kano model: Professor Noriaki Kano initially introduced a two-factor quality model, commonly known as the "Kano Curve." This curve illustrates the difference between the first quadrant "attractive quality," the second quadrant "unexpected quality" (thrilled customer), and the third quadrant "must-be quality." These categories were originally developed in 1984 by the Japanese quality expert Noriaki Kano.

KM: knowledge management.

KPI: key performance indicators.

KPMG: a global professional firm providing audit, tax, and advisory services.

Lean: a methodology for reviewing the way we conduct our everyday business activities, focusing on the processes and not the people.

Lean daily management system (5s+2): a system involving principles of sort, stabilize, shine, standardize, sustain plus safety and scheduled maintenance.

Leadership Academy: an in-house facilities planning and management leadership academy to provide the requisite compulsory and needed training for all staff.

Lean Manufacturing: simply referred to as LEAN, used as an optimal process improvement standard for producing goods and services through removal of waste. This generic philosophy was derived from Toyota Production Systems, which removed seven waste items to improve customer value.

Lean Sigma: integrated Lean and Six Sigma processes; a quality industry terminology used by many corporations.

LT: lead time, the total time a customer must wait to receive a product or service after placing an order.

LTP: lean thinking principles.

MAIC: measure, analyze, improve, and control.

MBNQA: the Malcolm Baldrige National Quality Award, established in 1987.

MEM: microelectromechanical machine, smaller than dust mites and formed out of microscopic gears, chains, and computer chips.

Metrics: A metric is a standard unit of measure or a set of ways to quantitatively measure, assess, control, or select a person, process, event, or institution, along with the procedures to carry out measurements in each of the activities. In this book, the term *metrics* is used to focus on the idea that "you measure what you value." That is, an individual or an organization would use the appropriate metrics tools allowing the most significant impact of the effectiveness and operational excellence of an organization through the above-mentioned parameters.

MOM: moment of magic.

MOT: moment of truth.

MTBF: mean time between failures.

MTS: meeting specifications.

Muda: the Japanese word for *waste*, which, when applied to management of the workplace, refers to a wide range of non-value-added activities, activities that result in waste that must be eliminated. According to Shiego Shingo, there are seven kinds of *muda*: (1) excess production and too-early production; (2) delays; (3) unnecessary movement and transport; (4) poor process design; (5) excessive inventory of items not in demand; (6) inefficient performance of a process; and (7) the making of defective items. However, Taiichi Ohno's enumeration differs slightly in categorizing the waste commonly found in the physical production: (1) overproduction ahead of demand, waiting for the next step; (2) unnecessary transportation of material between functional areas of facilities; (3) overprocessing of parts due to poor tools and design; (4) maintaining inventory amounts of more than the absolute minimum; (5) unnecessary movement by employees during the course of their work; and (6) defective parts.

Nanorobots (nanobots, nanoids, or nanites): very small devices ranging in size from 0.1 to 10 micrometers, first introduced in concept by the renowned physicist Richard P. Feynman (1918–1988), who was known for the path integral formulation of quantum mechanics, the theory of quantum electrodynamics, the physics of the superfluidity of supercooled liquid helium, as well as his work in particle physics.

NASULGC: the National Association of State Universities and Land-Grant Colleges.

Near perfection: tending to zero waste with high quality and fast delivery.

NEM: numerical evaluation of metrics.

NEO: new employee orientations.

NGO: nongovernmental organization.

NIH: not invented here.

NIST: National Institute of Science and Technology.

OCT: organized creative technology.

OLA: Operational Leadership Academy.

Operational excellence: to create a world-class operation with organizational effectiveness, facilities planning and management's process had to be operationally excellent in all areas of manufacturing or commercial activities.

Operational Specifications: the ISO 9000 standard comes closest to describing documentation of procedures so that unbiased, repeatable standardization occurs.

OPM: one plus more.

OR: operation research.

Organizational effectiveness: based on the percentage of billable hours for each unit per fiscal year, the business entities calculation uses the standard of 2,088 work hours of productive employment per annum per employee. How each worker performs producing a unit product or how each organization performs in its entirety. Like organizations can make comparative analysis to determine how effective they are compared to the competition, given the same circumstances and workplace conditions.

Pareto chart: a graphical tool for ranking from the most significant cause to the least significant, it is based on the Pareto Principle first defined by J. M. Juran named after the nineteenth-century Italian economist Vilfredo Pareto. This principle is used for analyzing data for sorting out the trivial many and the vital few bits of information in determining which project to select. It is based on the 80/20 rule: the principle that 80 percent of a problem can be attributed to the other 20 percent.

Pathfinding: finding a direction, leading the pack.

Pathing: career track.

PDCA: plan, do, check, act (Shewart cycle and Deming's model).

PDSA: plan, do, study, act.

Peer institutes (for Iowa State University): these include Michigan State University, North Carolina State University, Ohio State University, Purdue University, Texas A&M University, the University of Arizona, the University of California-Davis, the University of Illinois, the University of Minnesota, and the University of Wisconsin.

Perception check: regularly scheduled individual meetings with the associate vice president. These one-on-one meetings with an employee and the AVP are for mentoring and the continuous improvement message of attaining a world-class stature.

Petaflop: a measure of a computer's processing speed; it can be expressed as a thousand trillion floating-point operations per second.

Pissed-off line: the bottom line of customer tolerance. Customers get "pissed off" if they do not get the minimum requirements they expect. An organization needs to elevate its operational excellence up the ladder at least to the "should be zone" or the "future state" to become an average world-class operation. The "is" from the pissed-off line refers to the "as is" conditions that exist in any operation that needs to be mapped using value stream mapping to find out what to do to get to the next step.

Pitch: the rate of customer demand or Takt time.

PM: project management/manager.

PMMME: people, machine, method, material, and environment.

Poka-yoke: error proofing.

Policy deployment: methods used to be sure that everyone in an organization is working effectively toward the same end.

P, PC: production, production capability.

PPM: parts per million.

PR: public relations.

Process focus: organizational emphasis is on "What made the process error?" instead of "Who made the error?"

Process owners: staff involved with actual hands-on process work, on-line supervised or self-directed teams performing tasks.

Productivity: measure of output or outcome.

Profit: price – costs, a new paradigm that is market driven.

Pull systems: a manufacturing planning system that can be applied to the services sector based on communication. Generally known as the "pull concept," this is a just-in-time approach strategy whereby upstream production is only made as great as the needs of the downstream customer or consumer.

Push: old-school thinking whereby a sales forecast is developed and a product and/or service is produced, without taking into account whether or not there is truly enough demand to absorb it.

RCES: responsive, centered, empowered system.

RCI: rapid continuous improvements.

Reengineering: the mechanism that drives the time-based competition; redesign every process and move it closer to customer demand rate or Takt time.

ROI: return on investment.

RRT: rapid response time.

SA: situational analysis, the cultural assessment of an organization.

Safety: life safety.

Scenario planning: a strategic planning method that some organizations use to make flexible long-term plans.

SCUP: Society of College and University Planners.

SD: standard deviation.

Self-study: the self-assessment of an organization to determine its strengths and weakness and to provide a guide for evaluation by external examiners to comment or make recommendations for improvements.

Senior leaders: Leadership in any organization that helps the strategically focused organization to navigate through time.

Should be: the desired future state of an operation with an average or 3-Sigma level.

Silo: a concept that refers to each unit operating on its own without cross-functional connections. Silo thinking, silo vision, silo mentality, or the silo effect is the result of internal functional barriers. Silos are evident when directors, departments, managers, teams, or staff may be high performers individually, but may fail to choreograph or coordinate theirvarious activities to create peak performance for the organization.

SIPOC: supplier, input process, outcome, and customer.

Six Sigma: commonly defined as 3.4 defects per million opportunities. Six Sigma can be defined and understood at three distinct levels: metric, methodological, and philosophical.

SPC: statistical process control.

SQC: statistical quality control.

STEP: trends which are key driving forces.

SWOT: strengths, weaknesses, opportunities, and threats.

SSM: Society for the Sisters of Mary; the first national healthcare Baldrige award winner.

TAG: training and advisory group.

Takt time: From the German term *Takt*, meaning "rhythm." Takt time is the allowable time to produce one product at the rate that customers are demanding (the demand rate).

TEFMA: Tertiary Education Facilities Management Association.

Teraflop: one trillion floating-point operations per second.

TFM: total facilities management.

TOC: the Theory of Constraints as developed by Eliyahu Goldratt, an Israeli physicist/economist. Eliyahu M. Goldratt (1948–) is an Israeli physicist turned business consultant. He is the originator of the Theory of Constraints (TOC) and Critical Chain Project Management (CCPM). He claims to have applied the scientific method to resolving some of the permanent problems of organizations.

TPM: total preventative maintenance, the minimization of equipment downtime.

TPS: the Toyota Production System. The Toyota Production System (TPS) combines management philosophy and practices to form an integrated sociotechnical system at Toyota. The TPS organizes manufacturing and logistics for the automobile manufacturer, including interaction with suppliers and customers. The system is a major precursor of the more generic "Lean manufacturing." Taiichi Ohno, Shigeo Shingo, and Eiji Toyoda developed the system between 1948 and 1975. Originally called "Just In Time Production," it builds on the approach created by the founder of Toyota, Sakichi Toyoda, his son Kiichiro Toyoda, and the engineer Taiichi Ohno. The founders of Toyota drew heavily on the work of W. Edwards Deming and the writings of Henry Ford.

TRIZ: the Theory of Inventive Problem Solving. The analytical, left-brain creativity method that works exceedingly well in the analytical world beyond Six Sigma. It also is described as the "theory of solving inventors' problems" or "the theory of inventors' problem solving." It was developed by a Soviet engineer and researcher, Genrich Altshuller, and his colleagues starting in 1946. It has been evolving ever since. (The acronym *TRIZ* is derived from the original Russian phrase.) Today, TRIZ is a methodology, tool set, knowledge base, and model-based technology for generating innovative ideas and solutions for problem solving. TRIZ provides tools and methods for use in problem formulation, system analysis, failure analysis, and patterns of system evolution (both "as-is" and "could be"). However, I put this in a higher plane in solving innovative and inventive problems at beyond the "could be" level (beyond six sigma). TRIZ, in contrast to techniques such as brainstorming (which is based on random idea generation), aims to create an algorithmic approach to the invention of new systems, and the refinement of old systems.

Trough of chaos: reorganizational change transformation sigmoid curve.

Value: the value a customer feels as compared to value-added and non–value-added work performed.

VMV: values, mission, vision.

VOC: voice of the customer.

VOE: voice of the employee.

VSM: value stream manager.

VSM: value stream mapping.

Waiting: waiting for activities to occur.

Waste: The Japanese word *muda*, for "waste"; when applied to the workplace it refers to a range of non-value-added activities.

Webbify: putting activities on Web pages. Terminology developed by the author during implementation of Web pages before the 12-year journey started to leverage technology to make process improvements. Currently, the author's organization has

1,299 web pages on the internal site, and 1,410 on the external site, for a total of 2,709 total web pages.

WIP: work in progress.

Workflow: A workflow is a depiction of a sequence of operations in the process of an organization. This includes the assignment of work to a person, work to a group of persons, work to the subunit of an organization or staff, or work assigned to machines. Workflow may be seen as any abstraction of real work, segregated in work share, work split, or whatever types of assignments are involved as an outcome of customer demand. In a manufacturing sector or commercial enterprise for control purposes, workflow may be seen as a view of work under a chosen aspect to remove flaws or improve production.

Workforce engagement: the state of being committed, emotionally and intellectually, to accomplishing the work of an organization in support of its values, mission, and vision.

Workforce system: how the work of an organization is accomplished; core competencies.

WKE: we know everything.

Yield: output measured in percentage.

Y2K: the year 2000.

Zytec: industry leader in the 1990s for customer and market segmentation. The company was started in 1984 profiling customers and determining customer satisfaction parameters. Zytec's focus was product quality, measured in parts per million, and product reliability, measured in mean time between failures.

Bibliography

Ahoy, Christopher K. "Creating a World-Class Operation." National and International Lectures Presentation Series, 1997–2007.

Ahoy, Christopher K. "Leadership in Educational Facilities Administration," APPA, 2007.

Ahoy, Christopher K. "From the Desk of Chris Ahoy Series." Facilities Planning and Management, Iowa State University, News Bulletin articles, 1997–2007, available at http://www.fpm.iastate.edu.

APPA. "Maintenance and Staffing Guidelines for Educational Facilities," APPA, 2002.

Albright, Karl, with the TQS group. *The Only Thing That Matters: Bring the Power of the Customer into the Center of your Business*, Harper Business, 1992.

Altshuller, Genrich, with new material by Lev Shulyak. Translated and edited by Lev Shulyak and Steven Rodman. *40 Principles— TRIZ Keys to Technical Innovations*, Technical Innovation Center, 1994.

Baldrige National Quality Program, NIST. *Leadership Criteria for Performance Excellence*, available at www.baldrige.nist.gov.

Barker, Joe Arthur. *Paradigms: The Business of Discovering the Future*, HarperCollins, 1992.

Barrett, Richard. *Building a Values-Driven Organization: A Whole System Approach to Cultural Transformation*, Elservier–Sabre Foundations, 2006.

Barney, Matt, and McCarthy, Tom. *The New Six Sigma: A Leader's Guide to Achieving Rapid Business Improvement and Sustainable Results*, Prentice Hall, 2003.

Bash, Michael D. *Customer Culture: How FedEx and Other Great Companies Put the Customers First Every Day*, Prentice Hall, 2002.

Belasco, James A., and Stayer, Ralph C. *Flight of the Buffalo: Soaring to Excellence, Learning to Let Employees Lead*, Warner Books, 1993.

Blanchard, Ken, and Waghorn, Terry. *Mission Possible: Becoming a World-Class Organization While There Is Still Time*, McGraw-Hill, 1997.

Bossidy, Larry. *Execution: The Discipline of Getting Things Done*, Crown, 2002.

Brassard, Michael, and Ritter, Diane. *Sailing through Six Sigma: How the Power of People Can Perfect Processes and Drive Down Costs*, Brassard and Ritter, 2001.

Brown, Mark Graham. *Keeping Score: Using the Right Metrics to Drive World-Class Performance*, Quality Resources, AMACIM, 1996.

Bridges, William. *Managing Transitions: Making the Most of Change*, Addison-Wesley, 1991.

Brue, Greg. *Six Sigma for Managers*, McGraw-Hill, New York, 2002.

Buckingham, Marcus, and Clifton, Donald O. *Now Discover Your Strengths*, Free Press, 2001.

Chowdhury, Subir. *The Power of Six Sigma*, Dearborn Trade, 2001.

Cialdini, Robert B. *Influence: Science and Practice*, Allyn & Bacon, 2000.

Clifton, Donald O., and Nelson, Paula. *Soar with Your Strength*, Dell, 1992.

Collins, James C., and Porras, Jerry I. *Built to Last: Successful Habits of Visionary Companies*, HarperCollins, 1994.

Collins, Jim. *Good to Great*, HarperCollins, 2001.

Cornesky, Robert; McCool, Sam; Brynes, Larry; and Weber, Robert. *Implementing Total Quality Management in Higher Education*, Magna Publications, 1992.

Covey, Steven. *The Seven Habits of Highly Effective People: Restoring the Character Ethic*, Simon & Schuster, 1989.

Covey, Steven. *The Eighth Habit: From Effectiveness to Greatness*, Free Press, 2004.

Dyer, Wayne, W. *Change Your Thoughts, Change Your Life: Living with the Wisdom of Tao*, Hay House, 2007.

Eckes, George. *The Six Sigma Revolution: How General Electric and Others Turned Process into Profit*, John Wiley, 2001.

Fischer, Donald C. *Measuring Up to the Baldrige: A Quick and Easy Self-Assessment Guide for Organizations of All Sizes*, American Management Association, 1998.

Fuller, Buckminster. *The Critical Path*, St. Martin's Press, 1981.

George, Michael L. *Lean Six Sigma: Combining Six Sigma Quality with Lean Speed*, McGraw-Hill, 2002.

George, Michael L. *Lean Six Sigma for Service: How to Use Lean Speed and Six Sigma Quality to Improve Services and Transactions*, McGraw-Hill, 2003.

Hammel, Gary. *Leading the Revolution*, Plume Books, 2002.

Hammer, Michael, and Champhy, James. *Reengineering the Corporations: A Manifesto for Business Revolutions*, Collins Business Essentials, 2006.

Hanna, David P. *Designing Organizations for High Performance*, Addison Wesley, 1988.

Harrington, James H. *Business Process Improvement: The Breakthrough Strategy for Total Quality Productivity, and Competitiveness*, McGraw-Hill, 1991.

Harry, Mikel, and Schroeder, Richard. *Six Sigma: the Breakthrough Management Strategy Revolutionizing the World's Top Corporations*, Doubleday Currency, 2000.

Hawkins, David R. *Power vs. Force: The Hidden Determinants of Human Behavior*, Hays House, 1995, 1998, 2002.

Heider, John. *The Tao of Leadership: Lao Tzu's Tao Te Ching Adapted for a New Age*, Humanic New Age, 1985.

Hutton, David H. *From Baldrige to the Bottom Line: A Road Map for Organizational Change and Improvement*, ASQ, 2000.

Ishakawa, Kaoru, translated by David J. Lu. *What Is Total Quality Control? The Japanese Way*, Prentice-Hall, 1985.

Juran, J. M. *Juran on Leadership for Quality: An Executive Handbook*, Free Press, 1989.

Juran, J. M. *Juran on Quality by Design: The New Steps for Planning Quality into Goods and Services*, Free Press, 1992.

Kaplan, Robert S., and Norton, David P. *Balanced Scorecard: Translating Strategy into Action*, HBS Press, Simon & Schuster, 1996.

Keen, Peter W. *The Process Edge: Creating Values Where It Counts, How Firms Thrive by Getting Right Process Right*, Harvard Business School Press, 1997.

Kotter, John P. *Leading Change*, Harvard Business School Press, 1996.

Nalebuff, Barry, and Ayres, Ian. *Why Not? How to Use Everyday Ingenuity to Solve Problems Big and Small*, Harvard Business School Press, 2003.

Omachounu, Vincent K., and Ross, Joel E. *Principles of Total Quality*, St. Lucie Press, 1994.

Pande, Peter S.; Nueman, Robert P.; and Cavanaugh, Roland R. *The Six Sigma Way: How GE, Motorola and Other Top Companies Are Honing Their Performance*, McGraw-Hill, 2000.

Patterson, Kerry; Grenny, Joseph; McMillan, Ron; and Switzler, Al. *Crucial Conversations, Tools for Talking When Stakes Are High*, McGraw-Hill, 2002.

Peterson, Erick. "Seven Revolutions—Scanning the World Out to 2025," Webcast sponsored by CSIS Center for Strategic and International Studies, The New York Times, Knowledge Network, and SCUP Society for College and University Planners, March 2008; related material available online at www.CSIS.org under title "Scanning the Horizon: An Assessment of Critical Global Trends."

Ross, Alan M. *Beyond World Class: Building Character, Relationships, and Profit*, Dearborn, 2002.

Scott, Dru. *Customer Satisfaction, Practical Tools for Building Important Relationships*, third edition, Fifty Minutes Series Book, Crisp Publications, 2000.

Seidman, Dov. *How We Do Anything Means Everything in Business and in Life*, John Wiley, 2007.

Snee, Ronald D., and Hoerl, Roger W. *Leading Six Sigma: A Step-by-Step Guide Based on Experience with GE and Other Six Sigma Companies*, Prentice Hall, 2003.

Star, Harold, and Snyder, Stephen. *Understanding the Essentials of the Six Sigma Quality Initiative*. Quality Management Group, 2000.

Tague, Nancy R. *The Quality Toolbox*, second edition, ASQ Quality Press, 2005.

Total Quality Tools, version 2, Productivity-Quality Systems Inc., November 1996.

Walton, Sam, and Huey, John. *Sam Walton: Made in America*, Doubleday, 1992; Bantam, 1993.

Weber, Austin. "Nanotech: Small Products, Big Potential," *Assembly Magazine*, February 5, 2004, available online at www. assemblymag.com/CDA/ArticleInformation/features/BNP__ Features__Item/0,6493,118358,00.html.

Wheatley, Margaret. *Finding Our Way: Leadership for an Uncertain Time*, Berrett-Koehler, 2005.

Wherrett, Carl, and Yelovich, John. "Profiting from Nanotechnology," *The Motley Fool*, February 24, 2004, available at www.fool.com/news/commentary/2004/commentary040224wy.htm.

Wilber, Ken. *Theory of Everything*, Shambhala, 1996.

Womack, James P., and Jones, Daniel T. *Lean Thinking: Banish Waste and Create Wealth in Your Corporation*, Simon & Schuster, 1996.

Zeitz, Paul. *The Art and Craft of Problem Solving*, John Wiley, 2006.

Index